Eyewitness
COMPUTER

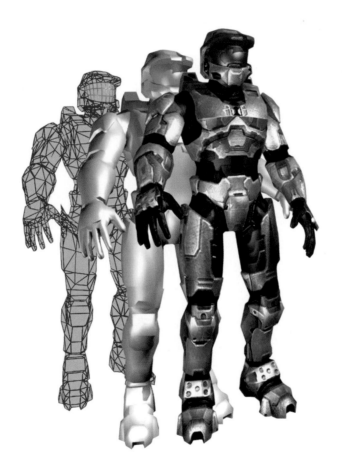

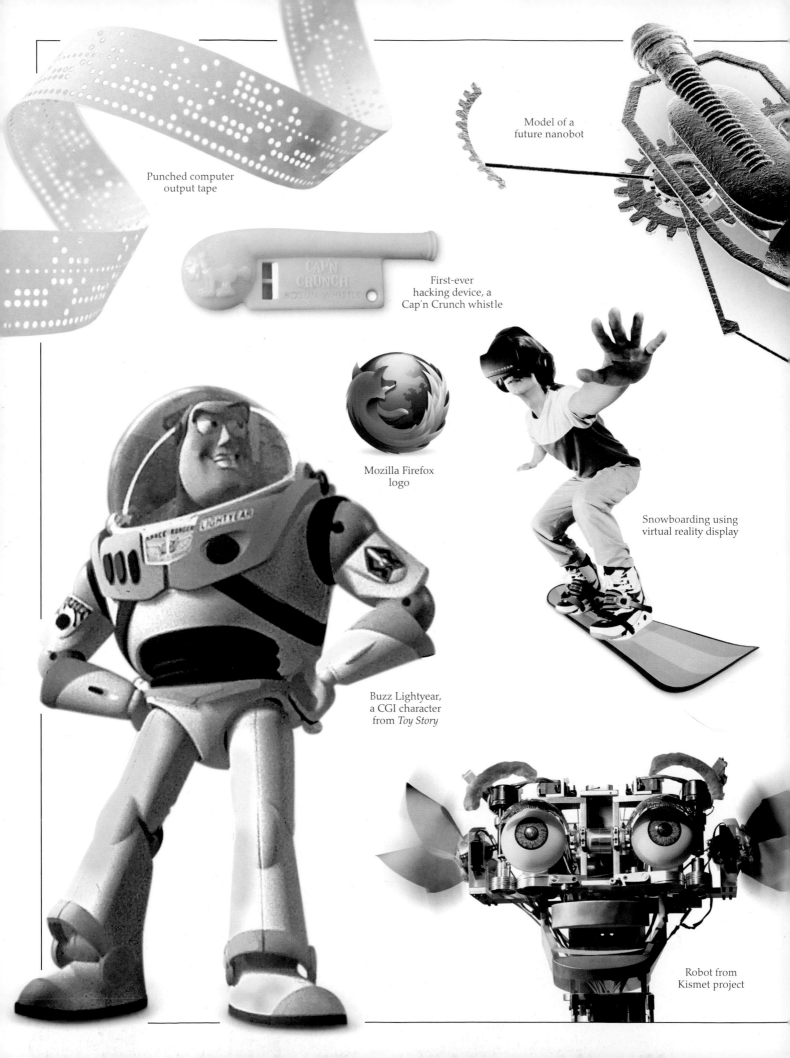

Punched computer
output tape

Model of a
future nanobot

First-ever
hacking device, a
Cap'n Crunch whistle

Mozilla Firefox
logo

Snowboarding using
virtual reality display

Buzz Lightyear,
a CGI character
from *Toy Story*

Robot from
Kismet project

Eyewitness
COMPUTER

Random access memory

Written by
Dr. Mike Goldsmith
and
Tom Jackson

Microprocessor

DK

DK Publishing

Pac-Man
eating dots

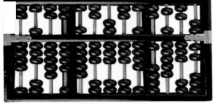

Chinese abacus

**LONDON, NEW YORK,
MELBOURNE, MUNICH, AND DELHI**

Consultant Dr. Jon Woodcock

DK DELHI

Project editor Kingshuk Ghoshal
Project art editor Govind Mittal
Editor Virien Chopra
Assistant art editor Nishesh Bhatnagar
Senior DTP designer Tarun Sharma
DTP designer Mohammad Usman
DTP manager Sunil Sharma
Managing editor Suchismita Banerjee
Managing art editor Romi Chakraborty
Production manager Pankaj Sharma

DK LONDON

Senior editor Rob Houston
Senior art editor Carol Davis
Associate publisher Andrew Macintyre
Picture researchers Jenny Faithful,
Sarah Hopper, Myriam Mégharbi
Production editor Andy Hilliard
Production controller Charlotte Oliver
Jacket designer Neal Cobourne
US editor Margaret Parrish

First published in the United States in 2011
by DK Publishing, 375 Hudson Street
New York, New York 10014

Copyright © 2011 Dorling Kindersley Limited
10 9 8 7 6 5 4 3 2 1
001—178346—Jul/11

A catalog record for this book is available from the Library of Congress.

ISBN 978-0-7566-8265-1 (Hardcover)
978-0-7566-8266-8 (Library binding)

Color reproduction by MDP, UK
Printed and bound by Toppan Printing Co. (Shenzhen) Ltd., China

www.dk.com

Thermionic valve

Layered view of
hard disk drive

Exoskeleton

Contents

Touchscreen

Genghis robot

What is a computer?

IT IS PERHAPS SURPRISING, considering how many people use computers in their everyday lives, that so few of us really know what a computer is, or how it works. A computer is a device that can follow a set of instructions—or a program. Computers can follow any program written in the right code, and modern computers can run many, seemingly at the same time. They are the most versatile tools ever invented. A musician can create a music album with a computer without playing a note and then share it with the world at the touch of a button, while a fighter jet can make impossible turns thanks to computers. They have changed the way we live, and in the future they will change it in ways we cannot yet imagine.

HUMAN COMPUTERS
The first use of the word computer was not for a machine but for a person! The word dates from the 17th century and actually referred to an expert mathematician who calculated complex sums. In the 1940s, the Dryden Flight Research Center (a forerunner of NASA) was testing its supersonic planes and space rockets and was collecting a vast amount of information, or data. The data was analyzed by humans—mostly women—who came to be called computers. They wrote everything on paper and used mechanical calculators called slide rules.

Screen display created by software running on computer

FOUNDING FIGURE
British mathematician Alan Turing is regarded as the founder of computer science. He was key to refining the idea of an algorithm—a mathematical way of solving problems in a series of steps—and developing it into a system of rules for handling data in computers. Every computer program uses many algorithms to work. In the 1930s, Turing described how a device could read and change bits of data by following an algorithm. This "Turing Machine," although only an idea, was able to show how computers might work.

Wireless mouse sends computer input by infrared

HOUSEHOLD MACHINES
Early computers were immense machines that filled entire rooms. The first personal computers in the 1970s were also boxlike and covered in lights and buttons (see page 12). By the 1990s, computers did not look out-of-place in a living room. This 2010 computer's microprocessor and memory (see pages 14–15) are hidden behind the screen. These physical parts make up the computer's hardware, but they are useless without software—the set of programs that tells them what to do (see pages 32–35).

Display screen with remote control, keyboard, and mouse

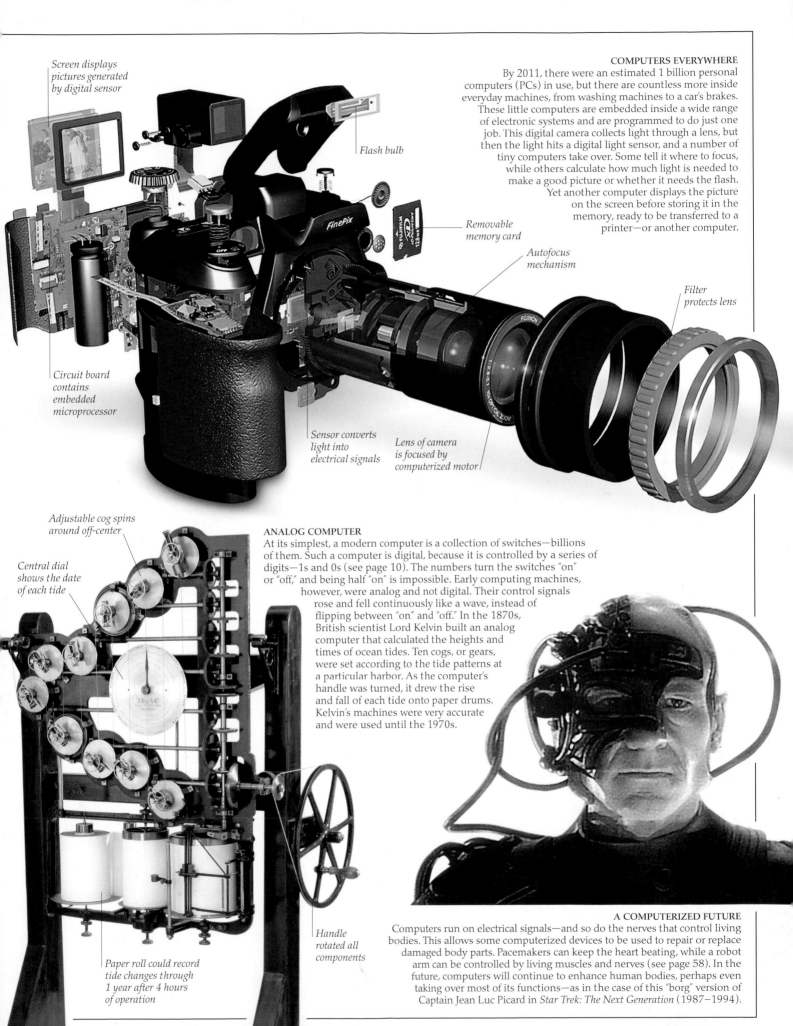

Screen displays pictures generated by digital sensor

Flash bulb

COMPUTERS EVERYWHERE

By 2011, there were an estimated 1 billion personal computers (PCs) in use, but there are countless more inside everyday machines, from washing machines to a car's brakes. These little computers are embedded inside a wide range of electronic systems and are programmed to do just one job. This digital camera collects light through a lens, but then the light hits a digital light sensor, and a number of tiny computers take over. Some tell it where to focus, while others calculate how much light is needed to make a good picture or whether it needs the flash. Yet another computer displays the picture on the screen before storing it in the memory, ready to be transferred to a printer—or another computer.

Removable memory card

Autofocus mechanism

Filter protects lens

Circuit board contains embedded microprocessor

Sensor converts light into electrical signals

Lens of camera is focused by computerized motor

ANALOG COMPUTER

At its simplest, a modern computer is a collection of switches—billions of them. Such a computer is digital, because it is controlled by a series of digits—1s and 0s (see page 10). The numbers turn the switches "on" or "off," and being half "on" is impossible. Early computing machines, however, were analog and not digital. Their control signals rose and fell continuously like a wave, instead of flipping between "on" and "off." In the 1870s, British scientist Lord Kelvin built an analog computer that calculated the heights and times of ocean tides. Ten cogs, or gears, were set according to the tide patterns at a particular harbor. As the computer's handle was turned, it drew the rise and fall of each tide onto paper drums. Kelvin's machines were very accurate and were used until the 1970s.

Adjustable cog spins around off-center

Central dial shows the date of each tide

Handle rotated all components

Paper roll could record tide changes through 1 year after 4 hours of operation

A COMPUTERIZED FUTURE

Computers run on electrical signals—and so do the nerves that control living bodies. This allows some computerized devices to be used to repair or replace damaged body parts. Pacemakers can keep the heart beating, while a robot arm can be controlled by living muscles and nerves (see page 58). In the future, computers will continue to enhance human bodies, perhaps even taking over most of its functions—as in the case of this "borg" version of Captain Jean Luc Picard in *Star Trek: The Next Generation* (1987–1994).

Before computers

FOR THOUSANDS OF YEARS, people have invented machines to simplify mathematical calculations. The abacus first appeared in Mesopotamia around 2700 BCE. The ancient Greeks built mechanical devices capable of solving particular mathematical problems and, by the 17th century, people were using craftsmanship, developed while building mechanical clocks, to make complicated calculating machines. For many centuries, these machines could do no more than give the answer to a particular equation. In the 19th century, Charles Babbage came up with the idea of a machine that could do many kinds of calculation by following a whole series of instructions—which could be changed as required. Babbage called such machines analytical engines—we call them computers.

KEEPING COUNT
For many thousands of years, people have counted all kinds of things, from days to loaves of bread, and they have drawn or scratched lines, called tallies, on pieces of wood or bone to record the answers. This bone is over 20,000 years old and was found at Ishango in Africa. Scientists believe that people used it to record the phases of the Moon.

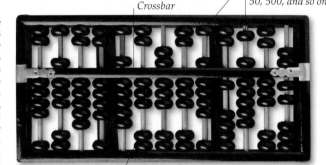

COUNTING BEADS
Invented more than 4,000 years ago, the abacus is one of the oldest calculating devices. In this 19th-century Chinese abacus, beads represent specific numbers. The column on the extreme right stands for the number of ones in a number, the column to its left is tens, the next, hundreds, and so on. The user enters numbers by sliding the beads toward the crossbar. The abacus is used to represent numbers, and also to perform calculations including addition, subtraction, division, and multiplication.

Beads above crossbar represent values of 5, 50, 500, and so on

Crossbar

Beads below crossbar represent values of 1, 10, 100, and so on

Chinese abacus

Each wheel represents one digit of a number

ANCIENT SKY TRACKER
The Antikythera mechanism is an amazingly advanced device built some time between 150 and 100 BCE, perhaps on the island of Rhodes. Divers recovered it in 1900 from a sunken Roman ship, which was wrecked off the island of Antikythera around 70 BCE. This device used a complicated arrangement of moving parts called gears (toothed wheels that interlock with one another) to calculate and display the positions of the Sun and the Moon, along with those of the major stars and perhaps also of the planets. It was so corroded by the sea that scientists needed many years of study to understand its function and mechanism. In 2007, a reconstruction of the device was presented to the National Hellinic Research Foundation in Athens, Greece. Incredibly, it worked perfectly.

STAR MACHINE

The Moorish astronomer Abu Ishaq Ibrahim al-Zarqali built this device—called an astrolabe—in about 1015 CE. Astrolabes were movable models of the sky. Ancient Greeks invented the earliest astrolabes in around 150 BCE, and such devices were in use in many countries until the 16th century CE. Astrolabes had many uses. If they were set with the position of a particular star over a place, or that of the Sun, they would display the time at that place. They also showed the stars that were visible at specific times from particular places on Earth. This probably helped travelers find out where they were. Astrolabes were a little like simple calculators, in that they displayed an answer on being fed with data.

Astrolabe is made of brass

Tympan, or backplate, shows which stars are above the horizon at a particular time

Rete is a movable plate labeled with the names of stars and turning it shows how the stars move over 24 hours

Toothed wheel forms part of interlocked gear network

Die-cast metal part

This square contains the fifth multiple of number on top square

Steel shaft supports columns

Dial on final column shows result of calculation

Single digit number in top square

NAPIER'S BONES

In 1617, John Napier invented a set of square columns called Napier's bones. Each bone was divided into nine squares, with the top square carrying a number between zero and nine. The squares below contained multiples of that number. Napier's bones helped perform multiplication and division. To multiply 548 by 5, for instance, a person would place these three bones on a board. The board had a column of nine squares on the left, marked 1–9. The user would then look at the squares on the bones that were next to the fifth position on the board. He or she would read the digits from left to right, adding the digits within the slanting lines. In this case, the answer would read as 2,740.

Napier's bones

CALCULATING TAX

The Pascaline was a mechanical calculator that could add or subtract numbers. Blaise Pascal, a philosopher and mathematician, developed the device in 1642 to help his father carry out calculations for taxation. The machine was quite difficult to use and so Pascal only managed to sell a few of them. However, the Pascaline spurred the development of more advanced devices, which finally led to the creation of the first computers.

Wheel used to input numbers

Number appears in slit to show result

DIFFERENCE ENGINE

In 1822, mathematician Charles Babbage built a prototype calculating machine, seen here. He used it to test out the working of a larger machine—Babbage's first Difference Engine—that he could not build due to a lack of funds. The engine used a system of gears to calculate tables of mathematical data. In 1991, the London Science Museum followed Babbage's plans and built the second Difference Engine—which worked perfectly. Babbage also designed—but did not build—what is considered by many to be the first true computer. Babbage called this the Analytical Engine. As a result, he is often known as the father of computing.

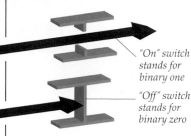

"On" switch stands for binary one

"Off" switch stands for binary zero

THE BINARY SYSTEM
Computers store and process data by setting electronic switches in different patterns, using a coding system called binary. An electronic switch can only be in two states—"on" and "off." In binary, the on state is number one and the off state is zero, as seen in this diagram of a binary switch. Groups of switches represent patterns of 1s and 0s, and these sequences in turn stand for numbers and letters. For example, 101 is the number five.

Electronic brains

WHEN COMPUTERS WERE STILL A NEW IDEA, they were such a marvel that people called them "electronic brains." It was the ability of a thermionic valve to switch an electric current on or off that became key to the development of the first generation of true computers, in the 1940s. These valves stored data in computers and performed calculations. Transistors were invented in 1947 and did the same job, but were smaller and more reliable. They heralded the second generation of computers.

Metal wire produced charged particles called electrons when heated

Valve of Colossus, an advanced electronic calculator

Metal plate received electrons that were attracted to it

CALCULATING WITH BINARY
The valves in early computers were connected together to form electronic circuits called logic gates that made calculations using binary numbers. The sums were used to process all kinds of data. Sums look very different in binary. 1+2=3 is written as 1+10=11. All computers still use logic gates and binary numbers.

A PIONEERING INVENTION
This is a false-color X-ray of a vacuum tube used in early radios. Early vacuum tubes, or thermionic valves, gave rise to the more complex ones used in computers. Thermionic valves can be used to stop or allow a flow of electricity, letting them act as switches. In first-generation computers, each valve switched one bit of data (see page 16). A series of valves stored data in the form of a sequence of 1s and 0s. As a program ran, the valves would switch on or off as the numbers they held changed. The valves could control each other and be built into useful computer circuits.

One of the 800 valves used in Pilot ACE

Console for controlling operations

SYSTEMS WITH VALVES
In 1950, computer pioneer Alan Turing built a valve-based computer called the Pilot ACE. It used 800 valves and helped scientists solve physics problems for many years. Bigger machines used far more valves. The AN/FSQ-7 was one of the largest computers ever built. Used by the US Air Force, it contained around 55,000 valves and weighed more than 245 tons (223 metric tons). The valves in such computers produced so much heat that they burned out and stopped the computers from working every few hours.

Pilot ACE

Terminal was electrified to put valve in "on" state

THE NEXT GENERATION

Like valves, transistors can also be used as switches. They work by using semiconductors—materials that carry an electric current sometimes, and block it at other times. Electricity flows into the transistor through one terminal and out through the second, but only if the transistor is switched on first by sending electricity through the third terminal. Transistors did what valves could, but were smaller, faster, cheaper, more reliable, and wasted less energy than valves. Transistors led to a whole new generation of faster computers, and tiny ones are present in most modern computer circuits.

Terminal of transistor

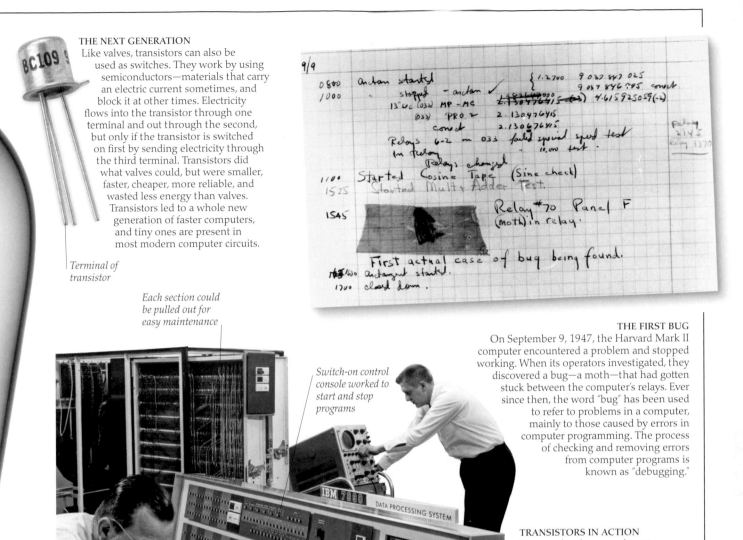

Each section could be pulled out for easy maintenance

Switch-on control console worked to start and stop programs

THE FIRST BUG

On September 9, 1947, the Harvard Mark II computer encountered a problem and stopped working. When its operators investigated, they discovered a bug—a moth—that had gotten stuck between the computer's relays. Ever since then, the word "bug" has been used to refer to problems in a computer, mainly to those caused by errors in computer programming. The process of checking and removing errors from computer programs is known as "debugging."

TRANSISTORS IN ACTION

It was only when people put transistors into computers in the 1950s that the machines became reliable enough to be really useful. Soon, several large companies began using them. International Business Machines (IBM), a computer-making company, tripled in size in the 1950s. American Airlines used an IBM 7090 computer (left) to reserve plane seats, carrying out the world's first online bookings in 1964.

Display screen for text and simple graphics

RUNNING FAST

Built by Control Data Corporation (CDC), the CDC 6600 was the first successful supercomputer (see pages 30–31), capable of performing more than 1 million instructions in a second—today's supercomputers can perform more than 1 quadrillion calculations in a second. This machine contained about 400,000 transistors based on the element silicon, instead of the germanium transistors that earlier computers used. More than 100 machines were sold, mostly to academic and military research laboratories. The CDC 6600 was the fastest computer in the world between 1964 and 1969.

Keyboard was used to select data for display or to change program

ALL ON BOARD
This is the world's first integrated circuit (IC), invented in 1958. It does the same job as a set of electronic components wired together, but in an IC, the parts are all built into the same unit and made of the same kind of material—called a semiconductor. A single IC can contain many transistors. These circuits are tough, compact, reliable, and can be mass-produced. ICs led to the development of smaller and more powerful machines, sometimes known as third-generation computers. These included cheap, compact machines called minicomputers.

Mini and micro computers

IN THE 1960S AND 1970S, computers rapidly became smaller and cheaper, thanks to two key electronic developments—the integrated circuit and the microprocessor. Each spurred the growth of a whole new generation of computers. The shrinking sizes and falling prices of computers changed the way people viewed these machines. Eventually, they appeared in schools and in homes. Computers changed from mysterious machines used only in some offices and laboratories to devices that were familiar—though still new and exciting. The development of cheap and powerful laptops since the 1980s has given people the freedom to use computers almost anywhere.

LANDING ON THE MOON
The Apollo spacecraft that took men to the Moon in the 1960s and 1970s were equipped with the first computers based on ICs. Although highly advanced for their time, they were less powerful than many of today's digital watches. But they were well programmed for the tasks they needed to perform. In 1969, the Apollo 11 spacecraft made the first-ever manned Moon landing. During the final stages of the landing, the computer in the spacecraft had to process so much information that it would have stopped working, had it not been specially designed to ignore less important tasks.

Astronaut Buzz Aldrin
on the Moon

*Pad connects microprocessor
to socket on the motherboard*

*Circuit board
performs processing*

MINICOMPUTERS
In the 1960s, minicomputers, such as the PDP-8, were developed as commercial computers. The first PDP-8s had individual transistors, but later versions used ICs. The PDP-8 went on sale in 1965 and was carefully designed to cost as little as possible. Its efficient design, along with its smaller size, made it very successful compared to other computers of the time—more than 50,000 units were sold.

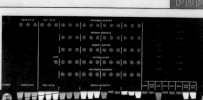

*Light displays output
and program status*

*Turning the key
started the PDP-8*

Intel Pentium P5
microprocessor,
1993–99

COMPUTERS FOR ALL
In 1981, the British Broadcasting Corporation (BBC) used this microcomputer in a TV series called *The Computer Programme*. Microcomputers were machines that used microprocessors and were part of the fourth generation of computers. Originally called the Acorn Proton, this computer was renamed the BBC Micro and was used in British schools in the 1980s. To display its output, users plugged it into a normal TV or specially made computer monitor (screen).

Monitor (screen) of Commodore PET

PET AT WORK
The Commodore PET was introduced in 1977 and was one of several microcomputers that came to be used widely in offices. At the time, most newly purchased computers required both time and skill to be set up, but the PET was ready to use as soon as it was plugged in. Its separate numeric keypad was unusual for the time and made it easier to enter data for scientific and business applications. It also quickly became a popular computer for home and school use.

Numeric keypad

LCD screen switches off automatically to save power if unused for a few minutes

Internal circuitry of microprocessor

Built-in cassette tape recorder used to save and load programs and data

Keyboard

Compact DVD drive

X-ray of a laptop

Battery

MICROPROCESSORS
During the 1960s, ICs became miniaturized until hundreds of transistors fit on a single piece, or chip, of silicon. These compact ICs became known as microchips. In 1971, Intel released its 4004 chip that performed the functions of a computer's central processing unit (see page 15) and was called a microprocessor. By 2010, microprocessors were driving every computer and contained as many as 2 billion transistors.

COMPUTERS ON THE MOVE
After microprocessors, the next leap forward in computer miniaturization was the development of portable laptops, or notebooks. These were all-in-one systems that incorporated many components, including the CPU, display, keyboard, and even speakers. The big challenge in developing laptops was to make screens that were small and light and that did not drain the batteries too quickly. The development of liquid crystal display (LCD) screens (see page 20) solved these problems. They use power very efficiently.

Inside a computer

Opening up a computer reveals a baffling array of electronic circuitry, but every computer has the same basic components. At the heart of the machine is the central processing unit (CPU), which controls most of its functions. In the 1970s, CPUs were first miniaturized onto a microchip called a microprocessor. Since that time, silicon-based chips also form the main memory of a computer—random access memory (RAM), which the CPU uses constantly when working. Computers also have long-term memory in the form of a storage device, such as a hard disk drive. Input and output devices (see pages 18–21) allow interaction with the user, while a computer's sensitive electronics require a smooth and constant power supply.

Fan blows cool air past fins

Metal fin removes excess heat

HOW COMPUTERS WORK
All computers work in the same way. When a user feeds data into them by an input device, the central processing unit (CPU), often a microprocessor, stores it in the memory. A program running in the memory then sends instructions to the CPU, which retrieves the data, processes it according to these instructions, and sends the results back to the memory. When required, the CPU transfers the processed data back to the user via an output device.

Memory

Central processing unit

Input

Output

KEEPING COOL
The electronic components of a computer run on a lot of electrical power and so generate heat. These parts are made of circuits that are sensitive to changes in temperature, and if they get too hot, the parts stop working properly. Devices called heat sinks help to get rid of this heat. Heat sinks take the form of metal fins that radiate heat away from the electronic parts to the air. A fan installed in the computer speeds up the cooling process by forcing warm air away from the fins, helping cooler air take its place.

DVD drive

Circuit board

ON THE INSIDE
Computers, such as this desktop machine from 2010, contain printed circuit boards, on which a microprocessor and other electronic parts are fixed and connected via copper tracks that are etched on to the board. Circuit boards are often provided with expansion slots to allow enthusiasts to add extra devices, such as graphics cards. Computer designers cram as much circuitry as possible into the available space, while allowing enough room for air to circulate so that heat can escape. Many parts are modular—they can be removed easily in one piece.

DISKS OF DATA
The computer dismantled here stores its data on a hard disk drive. To retrieve or store data, a magnetic head at the tip of an actuator arm moves rapidly across tiny areas on the disk's surface, or platter, as it spins at up to 15,000 revolutions per minute. To write data, the head magnetizes areas on the platter, which can be demagnetized for reuse. To read data from the disk, it converts the magnetic information into an electric current. Unlike data in the RAM, data stored on hard disk drives is not lost when the computer is switched off.

Metal cover protects magnetic disk

Platter of magnetic disk

Head of actuator arm reads and writes data

Chip controls actuator arm and rotation of disk

THE BRAIN

The CPU, mostly contained on a microprocessor, is the brain of every computer. It controls most of the machine's operations, transferring data to and from memory as required, processing it as instructed by software, and then either storing it back in memory or transferring it to the screen or other output device.

Microprocessor

Microchip can store as many as 1 billion binary bits

MEMORY POWER

Data that the computer is actively working on is stored in the RAM. In a 2010 desktop computer, the RAM is stored in a series of microchips on a RAM board. It is called random access memory because the computer can access any piece of it at any time. It writes the data to the memory in whatever pattern is quickest for it to use, rather than in a sequence a human would understand. So a single piece of data may be scattered over several microchips.

A HELPING HAND

Watching high-definition (HD) videos or playing modern video games on a computer requires a lot of memory and processing power, slowing down the computer. Graphics cards are printed circuit boards that contain a specialized microchip called a graphics processing unit (GPU). The GPU supplements the processing power of the CPU by taking over mathematical calculations for producing images. Graphics cards also have their own memory called video RAM (VRAM).

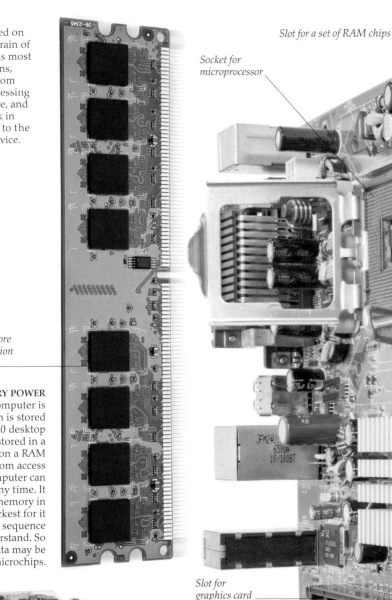

Slot for a set of RAM chips

Socket for microprocessor

Slot for graphics card

Backup battery

MOTHERBOARD

The main printed circuit board of a computer is called the motherboard. It contains the microprocessor and key components—including the backup battery and the basic input/output system (BIOS) chip. The battery keeps the computer's clock running while the computer is switched off. The BIOS chip carries the software that starts the operating system (see page 32) when the computer is switched on. The motherboard also contains slots for other devices, such as extra RAM chips and graphics cards.

BIOS chip

Tube contains mercury

MERCURY DELAY LINES

In the 1940s, some of the earliest electronic computers stored data in mercury delay lines in the form of sound waves. Delay lines were tubes filled with mercury, with a quartz crystal at each end. The computer wrote data to the tube as an electrical signal. This made one crystal vibrate, sending sound waves down the tube. The crystal at the other end turned the sound back into electrical signals, and these were fed back to the first crystal, which repeated the sound waves. As a result, the sounds did not die away until the delay line was switched off. A computer was connected to one end of the tube, but often had to wait for the required data to appear.

Magnetic data storage tapes in a rack, in a computer tape library

Cable transfers data to and from the delay line

Casing at end of line contains quartz crystal

Memory and storage

SINCE THE EARLIEST VALVE COMPUTERS, the basic approach to data storage has been the same. To store data, a computer sets many two-way electronic switches in a pattern representing 1s and 0s. Each digit is one "bit" of information, and eight bits compose one byte of data. When a program is run, this pattern changes. In the early days of computing, the data in a computer's memory was held in place by a constant power supply. It vanished when the computer shut down (it was called "volatile"), so the data could be captured permanently only by a printout. Later, engineers invented ways of storing electronic data with the power off. These non-volatile memory methods involve tapes, disks, and other media. Today's computers move data between their volatile memory (specifically, random access memory, or RAM) and their non-volatile stores, such as hard disks.

Bright dot represents a binary one and faint dot is a zero

Screen of Williams tube

Screen is covered by electrical grid

READING MEMORY

Random access memory (RAM) can be written randomly, or in any order. The Williams tube was the first RAM device. A computer stored data on it by shooting a beam of electrons on to its screen. The beam left electrically charged patches on the screen, each of which held one bit of data. An electrical grid on the front of the tube detected the charged patches, allowing the computer to read data in any order.

Data is fed to the tube in the form of electrical signals through a platform of connectors

Williams tube, 1946

STORE NOW, USE LATER

The magnetic tape is an early example of non-volatile memory. It was a popular storage medium from the 1950s to the 1980s and is still used sometimes. Earlier types were large spools of plastic tape with a metallic coating, which could be magnetized in patches, each representing one bit. Unlike the paper tapes that came before them, people could reuse magnetic tapes many times. Later versions stored tape in cassettes or cartridges, which were more compact and easier to handle. Though they can hold up to 3 terabytes (TB) of data, magnetic tapes are very slow because of the need to wind them to the section where the required data is written.

Laser writing to a DVD

OPTICAL DISKS

Some storage devices are removable. These include portable hard drives and optical disks, such as compact disks (CDs) and digital versatile disks (DVDs). Optical disks are popular because they are cheap, tough, and small, and can hold up to 17 gigabytes (GB) of data on a single disk. A red laser writes data to the disk by making pits (tiny impressions) on it at precise locations. The pits represent 0s and the smooth areas stand for 1s. The laser also reads data from the disk. Blu-ray disks (BDs) use a blue laser that makes smaller pits than on a DVD, allowing a BD to store seven times as much data as a DVD.

Metal casing encloses USB connector

Circuit board

Microchip acts as a bridge between USB connector and flash memory chip, which is on the other side of the drive

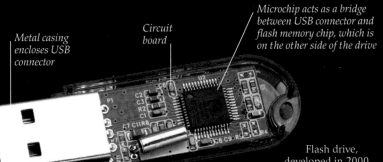

Flash drive, developed in 2000

Punched tape, used widely for data storage from 1950s to 1970s

A POCKET FULL OF DATA

A USB stick (also known as a flash drive, memory stick, or pen drive) is another example of non-volatile memory and a convenient type of removable data storage device. USB stands for universal serial bus, a type of socket found on almost every modern computer. A USB stick contains a flash memory chip that allows a computer to modify stored data much faster than on a hard drive. Flash drives are small enough to fit in a pocket, virtually shockproof, and, unlike a hard drive, contain no moving parts. Computers' CPUs can use both hard drives and USB sticks as "virtual memory," enhancing their RAM and speeding up their processing, but USB sticks are more efficient at this.

Hole on tape represents one bit of information

Pin connects the card to the computer or other device

MINIATURIZING MEMORY

Every year computers produce more data, but data storage technology has kept pace by packing data into smaller and smaller spaces. Some early electronic computers preserved data by outputting paper tape with holes punched in it, but this was bulky and easily damaged. Magnetic tapes could store far more data, but reading from or writing to them was still a slow process. In the 1980s, magnetic "floppy" disks made data access faster, although they could store only 1 or 2 megabytes of data—less than one compressed digital photograph from today's cameras. From around 1995, CDs and then DVDs—optical disks that could hold 1,000 times as much data—were introduced. By 2010, consumers could choose from a range of disks, compact cards, and microchip-based memory options, each offering many gigabytes of storage.

Memory card, developed in the early 1990s

Input

EVERY COMPUTER WORKS WITH INPUT—data and instructions that the user feeds into the computer so that it can begin its calculations. To enter data into the earliest computers, operators fed in cards or strips of film with holes punched in them. However, this was a very slow process suitable for inputting only words or numbers. Today computers can handle many different types of input—from text and sounds to radio signals, images, or even a touch. Some forms of input control the computer itself, while others feed data into programs for analysis. But first, all forms of input data need to be converted into electrical signals that a computer can process.

Finger disrupts electrical field at point of contact, shown by peak on mesh

Dial has two hands and counted the number of cards with the same pattern of holes

Electrical card reader contains pins that pass through holes in a card fed into it, allowing reader to recognize pattern of holes

Display changes according to touch input

COUNTING CARDS

Herman Hollerith's tabulating machines pioneered many of the principles that would later be adopted for computer input systems. His original device helped to analyze the data of the 1890 US census. The machine used an electrical card-reader to transfer information from punched cards to a series of counters. In this machine, the cards had to be fed in one by one, but later versions of the machine included automatic card-feeders, as well as systems to add and subtract data. Hollerith's Tabulating Machine Company later became the computer giant IBM.

Flap opens automatically, on a signal from the card reader, so human sorter can drop card into correct slot

KEYING IN

The QWERTY keyboard is the most common input device. Modern keyboards developed from the ones for typewriters. The keys in keyboards are not arranged in alphabetical order because, in the first typewriters, the mechanical keys easily jammed if those that were next to each other were typed in quick succession. So, the keys were arranged so that letters that are often used together are far apart. "QWERTY" spells out the letters that appear first in the sequence of keys.

Display unit

Card sorter

TOUCH AND TYPE

Touchscreen technology allows users to interact physically with what is shown on a screen. Inside the touchscreens of many computers and cell phones—such as this iPhone—is a glass layer coated with a grid of threads that conduct electricity. This grid generates an electrical field. When fingers touch the screen, the electrical field changes near the points of contact. The grid is connected to sensitive detectors that pinpoint the locations of these changes, creating a "map" of the touch input—the phone's computer uses this as its input data.

Balloon filled with hydrogen carries radiosonde

Protective layer on screen

Electrically charged touchscreen contains detectors that read disruption in electrical field and determine location of touch

Mesh is a representation of the electrical field

HOW'S THE WEATHER?

Not all input to computers comes from people. Some is sent directly by other devices, such as radiosondes. These measure weather conditions high above the ground and transmit information to weather stations by means of radio signals. A computer downloads this information for storage and analysis and uses it to generate weather forecasts. The computer also stores the time, location, and altitude at which the measurements were made.

Radiosonde

JOYSTICKS

Airplanes used the first joysticks about a century ago. Today, computers use joysticks for making fast and accurate movements with an on-screen cursor. Many computer games use these, too. Some joysticks have several buttons, allowing many functions to be controlled with one hand. Cranes and industrial assembly lines also make use of joysticks.

RECOGNIZING LANGUAGE

Computers recognize human speech by comparing it with data stored in a database. Spoken words have distinctive patterns of loudness and pitch, and a computer uses these patterns to identify words from their sounds. The computer can then convert this audio input into text that is displayed on the screen or a command to start an application.

Spike in waveform represents an instantaneously loud sound, such as abrupt "t" or "p"

Waveform representing human speech

MIGHTY MOUSE

The computer mouse was invented in 1963—the first mouse had wheels to move over a surface. Early models used a rubber ball beneath the device to track the movement of the mouse. A modern one uses optical sensors to detect movement, which is then translated into input signals. The mouse made it easy for users to navigate across the screen and select different items.

Output

COMPUTERS NEED OUTPUT DEVICES to relay the results of their calculations to their users. The printer is one of the earliest types. Printers were invented before computer screens and are still widely used. Display screens have developed from primitive, bulky, monochrome displays, to today's full-color flat-screen versions. Today, computers are used for many purposes and many more kinds of output device are available. Output data starts as electrical signals transmitted via wires or radio waves to these devices, which convert the signals into their different final forms.

Headphones

Soft foam covers the headphone speaker to protect ear

LISTENING IN
When a computer sends data to a headphone, it must first be converted from a digital form (in the form of binary code) to a varying pattern of electrical signals, which mimics that of a sound wave. In the headphone, the electrical pattern makes a metal plate, called a diaphragm, vibrate, and these vibrations travel through the air to the user's ear in the form of sound.

LIGHTING UP
Most computer screens in use today are liquid crystal displays (LCDs). The optical properties of liquid crystals can be controlled by electrical signals. LCDs contain thousands of tiny areas, called pixels. Every pixel is further divided into three sub-pixels. Each sub-pixel is covered with a red, green, or blue filter. When an electrical signal carrying picture data (a stream of numbers) is sent to a particular pixel, the liquid crystal changes to allow light to shine through a filter. The values in the data control the sub-pixels—in this case, the signal activates the green sub-pixels alone, producing the green color of the leaf.

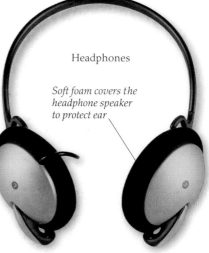

Red, green, and blue sub-pixels

Lens focuses beams of light

PROJECTED DATA

Projectors convert the flickering patterns of light that make up the output on a display screen into beams of light that can be projected onto any surface, such as a wall. There are many types of computer projectors, but most of them are based on LCD technology. Projectors are brighter than computer display screens and have a lens to focus the images sharply.

PAPER OUTPUT

Charles Babbage invented the first computer printer more than a century ago. Today, many kinds are available, each specialized for a particular use. This inkjet photo printer is designed to print images that are detailed, sharp, and brightly colored. But it is quite slow and uses a lot of ink. Laser printers are much faster but more expensive. Some devices combine printing, photocopying, and scanning functions in a single unit. Printers and other devices, such as image scanners and speakers, are known as peripherals.

Glossy paper makes image appear brighter

Speaker provides audio output

Navigation key

TOUCH AND READ

The BrailleNote Apex is an example of an output device for people who are visually impaired but can read an alphabet called Braille. This alphabet consists of patterns of bumps, each pattern being a different character. Readers trace their fingers over these bumps to recognize the characters. Rods inside the display terminal of this Braille device press up against the soft surface to create Braille characters. However, rather than being permanent like those in a printed book, the patterns change rapidly, providing the user with a flow of text, much like a computer screen. Eight thumb-sized buttons allow the user to access menus and files. This Braille device can also provide sound via speakers, offering another type of output to the user.

BrailleNote Apex

Braille output terminal

Original object

3-D digital model of object

PRINTING IN DEPTH

Ordinary printers output data on flat sheets of paper, but 3-D printers output solid objects. Users can either make shapes that are designed on-screen, or print 3-D copies of real objects that have been scanned in 3-D to create 3-D digital models. To do this, a laser first scans an object to determine its shape accurately. A computer program reconstructs this data into a digital model and converts it into thin slices. Finally, a 3-D printer outputs these slices in the form of shaped plastic sheets, laid on top of each other and stuck together.

Reproduction of object, made by 3-D printer

Wire connects to USB socket on computer

TEA TIME?

A computer often uses sockets termed universal serial bus (USB) to move or copy data to and from printers and other peripheral devices. In addition to transferring data, a computer can use these sockets to power devices. These can be small reading lights, cooling fans, or even novelty devices, such as this tea warmer. However, since USBs supply only 2.5 watts of power (an electric kettle uses 1,000 times more power), the warming effect is small.

Computers at work

FROM GUIDING MILITARY JETS through steep dives to predicting a rise in prices on the stock market, computers are at work everywhere. Computers can perform many tasks more accurately and efficiently than humans can. They can be programmed to store and process large amounts of data and they help storeowners to keep track of their stock. In many countries, people buy and sell goods not with paper money, but by telling computers to instruct banks to transfer money across computer networks. Computers can also track weather patterns and can sometimes predict weather conditions—with hit-and-miss success!

Robotic hand, or "end-effector," is specially designed for grasping files

Joint allows robot to reach the required position

Robot working in computer file room

FETCHING AND CARRYING
This robot has traveled down its track to a specific location in an immense storage facility to retrieve data on a cartridge of magnetic tape. How does it know where to go? It is connected to a computer containing a database of entries carrying the physical locations of each cartridge in the warehouse. Users needing the data make requests to the computer, which instructs the robot automatically. Banks of data like this can build up in archives of research facilities, such as particle accelerators (see page 31). However, robots and databases can be used in any large warehouse to retrieve anything that is stored there.

Pilot controls aircraft using a computer connected to sensors in aircraft

Jet performing a roll maneuver

Series of computer screens display stock prices across the globe

SHARE TRADING
In a stock market, people buy and sell shares in companies. Until the 1980s, share trading was done face-to-face on the busy trading floors of stock markets. But now, almost all share transactions take place over computer networks. Computers also analyze stock market data, providing information on the price of shares for traders to decide what to buy and when to sell.

STORM WARNING

In 2005, a computer generated this weather map using satellite images of Hurricane Rita. Computers that forecast the weather process a vast amount of data from multiple sources, such as satellites and weather stations. Using complex mathematical equations based on how the atmosphere behaves, these computers generate a list of possible weather forecasts. Although they are powerful, these computers cannot judge when they have gotten it wrong. Human weather forecasters need to step in and use common sense to choose which of the automatic weather forecasts is the most likely.

Yellow blip on radar screen represents an aircraft

LANDING AT SEA

From his position on an aircraft carrier at sea, an air traffic controller uses a computer to monitor the ship's 72 aircraft. The computer's input comes from a radar device that tracks the aircraft's movements. It uses this to display a map of aircraft positions on its screen. A database provides detailed background information about the aircraft, their 115 pilots, and their missions, and while in the air, each plane may be tagged with data, such as its identification, speed, and heading. The controller uses all this data to make sure the aircraft are always at safe distances and that there is space for them to land on the carrier. The computer also receives data from weather stations that allows the controller to warn pilots of approaching storms.

Flaperon on wing is controlled by the computer to bank the aircraft for changing direction

FLY-BY-WIRE

To achieve this stunt, engineers have made this F/A-18 Hornet jet fighter so unstable that a human pilot could not control it. This makes it more maneuverable, but it needs a computer to keep it flying. The computer receives input from motion sensors. It responds quickly to use this data to stabilize the aircraft, freeing the pilot to concentrate on tight turns and rolls. The pilot's joystick sends its movements as data to the computer, which transfers it to the control surfaces (rudder, flaps, and ailerons) by electrical wires, giving this technology the name "fly-by-wire." Most modern jet fighters and airliners now use fly-by-wire.

Bar code reader uses a laser to scan bar code data, which is then matched against a database

TAKING STOCK

A bottle of orange juice, like most items on sale in a supermarket, has a computer-readable bar code that is unique to it. These bar codes identify each item and allow the supermarket's computer system to keep track of all of its stock, from when it is bought until the moment it is sold. These systems not only indicate when supplies are running low, but they also check that the goods have not passed their sell-by dates and calculate profit, too.

Computers all around us

IN HIGH-TECH SOCIETIES, COMPUTERS AFFECT EVERY ASPECT of people's lives but often go unnoticed, working behind the scenes. Computers not only ensure that power plants supply power to homes, but they also monitor and control industrial output and traffic flow. Some are no more than tiny microprocessors built into gadgets, vehicles, and household appliances. These are called embedded computers and each one is designed to carry out a specific function very efficiently. Electronic devices that contain embedded computers, such as surveillance cameras, microchip identification tags, or ATMs, are usually linked to a more powerful computer that works to control and coordinate the operations of them all.

CAUGHT ON CAMERA

This surveillance camera has an embedded computer that automatically moves it to track vehicles or people crossing the camera's field of view. Authorities use these cameras to monitor crowds or traffic or to watch for criminal activity. A network of these cameras can help track stolen vehicles or even check if the driver has paid a toll (fee) to use the road. The computer identifies each car by its license plate—reading the characters by pattern recognition. It then checks with a database to see if the driver has paid the fee. In the future, the camera's computer could even be linked to a database of the faces of known criminals and could alert the authorities if it catches images of one.

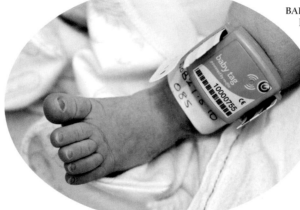

BABY WATCH

In some countries, computers keep track of people from the day they are born. The computerized tag on this newborn baby's leg contains data about the baby, such as its date of birth, weight, and the names of its parents. To protect it from the risks of kidnapping or misplacement, a microchip installed on the tag can locate the baby using a tracking system. Similar microchips can also help locate pet dogs and cats that have strayed from home.

Display shows speed

Display shows fuel status

Display shows total distance traveled

Suspicious object is marked as yellow blob by computer

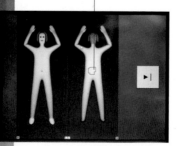

Scans of a passenger

SCANNING FOR SAFETY

Safety is a big concern today, especially during air travel. Many airports require that all travelers be searched. A whole-body scanner is a quick way of doing this. It uses radio waves that pass through clothing but reflect off the body and some objects that the traveler may be carrying. Different materials absorb and reflect radio waves in different ways and can be told apart. The computer in the booth measures the reflected waves to build an image from the scan. It processes the data and then highlights suspicious objects for investigation, as shown by the yellow blob superimposed on top of a "standard" image of a human being.

Control for audio system

LOOPING THE LOOP

Amusement park rides have to be safe as well as scary, and computers make sure they are. On roller coasters, sensors attached to the tracks monitor the location of all cars, enabling the ride's computers to activate emergency brakes if a breakdown leads to the risk of a collision. Computers also help design and test new rides.

CASH ON DEMAND

Before automated teller machines (ATMs) were introduced in the 1960s, people could only withdraw money by going to banks or post offices at particular times of day and waiting in long lines. Now money is available at any time at many more places. Every ATM contains a computer that is linked to a bank's central computer. The machine tracks the amount of money withdrawn by a user and automatically updates the user's bank account. The computer can also exchange currencies for users if they withdraw money in places with different currencies than their bank accounts.

TOYING WITH COMPUTERS

First launched in 1979, Big Trak is still available, making it the world's oldest computerized toy. It can be programmed to move a certain distance, fire its weapons, and then return to its original location. Many toys today contain embedded computers that allow the toys to respond to a spoken voice, touch, or light.

Control for regulating temperature

Navigation display uses information from GPS to instruct the driver how to reach destination

DIGITAL DRIVING

This dashboard of a Honda Insight car is packed with computer displays that provide data from different systems. Modern cars can have more than 50 embedded computers, which control most of the car's systems, including the brakes and throttle. Computers fine-tune the engine from second to second, making it run as efficiently as possible.

Track has switches and brakes that are controlled by computers

Gadgets on the go

Tape cassette

THERE ARE NEARLY AS MANY CELL PHONES in the world today as there are people. In the late 20th century, small, cheap computers revolutionized the world of gadgets, making them more powerful and versatile. These gadgets had a wide range of applications—MP3 players played music on the move, satellite navigation devices helped people find their way, and cell phones became "smart," enabling people to use them as pocket computers. Gadgets became popular, so manufacturers began to find ways of producing them cheaply to meet this demand. Today, more and more gadgets of many kinds can access the Internet (see pages 44–45), sending and receiving information all over the world in seconds.

MUSIC WHILE YOU WALK

The Sony Walkman was a popular music player in the 1980s. It used tape cassettes and let people listen to music anywhere. Today's MP3 players store music as digital data on flash drives (see page 17). Unlike tapes that need to be wound to the correct spot, flash drives can deliver any track the user desires and can store thousands of songs and pieces. The devices play MP3 files, whose data has been compressed so that it occupies only one-tenth of the space of raw sound data. MP3 players produce higher quality sound because storing music digitally eliminates noise, heard as tape hiss on Walkmans.

Icon for an application

TABLET COMPUTERS

Portable devices with touch-sensitive screens (see pages 18–19) emerged in 2010 as a new type of gadget—a tablet computer. A tablet computer can display a keyboard if needed. For other tasks, users can also use a pen-shaped instrument called a stylus. But for most tasks, users just use their fingers. Some tablet computers, such as the Apple iPad, register multiple touches at the same time. Multitouch technology makes it easy for the user to give input commands. For example, two fingers can be placed close together on an image on the screen and then drawn apart. The computer interprets this action as a zoom command and magnifies the image. The iPad is designed to work both as a personal computer and a media device—displaying movies, photos, and e-books.

Signal from first satellite helps calculate time difference between satellite and GPS receiver, which determines that the user must be somewhere on the green dotted line

Satellite 1

WHERE ARE YOU?

Many computerized gadgets contain receivers that can access the global positioning system (GPS), including tablet computers, cell phones, and digital watches. GPS uses a group of satellites in Earth orbit, each of which broadcasts a very accurate time signal using radio waves. A GPS device receives these signals and uses the timing information they carry to calculate its exact position. In reality, an extra fourth satellite signal is needed to help the GPS receiver check its own clock.

GOING MOBILE

Few people took cell phones seriously when they first appeared in the 1970s. They were large, heavy, and had short battery lives—and making calls on them was expensive and not very reliable. Since then, cell phones have become a global phenomenon and more than half the world's population has at least one. Early mobile phones had very little computer power, but during the 2000s, making phone calls on the move became only a tiny percentage of the devices' capability. Today's smart phone is a pocket computer with Internet access, camera, and music player, but it also happens to be a phone!

| *1982* Nokia Mobira Senator | *1984* Motorola DynaTAC 8000X | *1987* Nokia Mobira Cityman 900 | *1996* Motorola StarTac | *2002* Nokia 6310i | *2005* BlackBerry 7200 | *2007* Apple iPhone | *The near future* Nokia Morph concept phone |

COMPUTERS ON YOUR WRIST

The tiny computers embedded in digital watches have transformed them from simple timekeepers to gadgets that include calculators, video games, MP3 players, and digital cameras. Soon, some wristwatch-sized devices will be true computers, collecting data from their surroundings or from other devices and computers, or controlling remote systems by Wi-Fi (see page 43).

LCD screen displays the image almost instantly

Just one control is used to display and zoom in on stored photos, and to select from menus of options

SAY CHEESE!

The lenses in digital cameras focus incoming light on to a sensor that converts it into electrical signals. A computer then converts these signals into digital images. In a digital camera, the images can be edited or deleted and transferred easily from the camera to computers or other devices. Thousands can be stored on the camera itself—usually on a flash memory card.

Signal from second satellite narrows down user's location to one of the places where the blue and red dotted lines meet

Satellite 2

Satellite 3

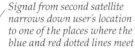

User's location is determined using signal from third satellite as the place where the three dotted lines meet

SHOWING THE WAY

Satellite navigation (sat-nav) devices are pocket-sized computers with a GPS receiver. They provide a map of the local area centered on the user's position. They do this by using GPS to determine the user's location on Earth's surface. In addition, they can work out routes to programmed-in destinations. Sat-navs carry out complex calculations when working out the shortest route between two places. They can also warn users of upcoming traffic problems.

Making computers

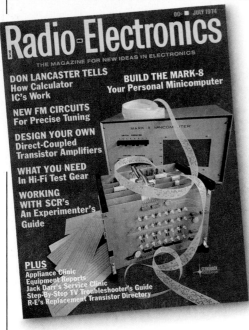

EARLY COMPUTERS WERE HAND-BUILT, constructed one at a time, and so expensive that only governments or huge companies could afford them. Computers for personal use had to be assembled at home and, for a long time, remained mainly a hobby. Today's computers are built rapidly on automated production lines—largely by robots—and in huge numbers, which is why these complicated devices are so affordable now. Computers store and process data on microchips, which are electronic circuits made by depositing chemical layers—in carefully etched patterns—on pieces of silicon. Microchips are much less delicate than older components such as valves, and so today's computers are also far more reliable and sturdier than ever.

MAKE YOUR OWN COMPUTER

The Mark-8 was a homemade computer built in 1973 by the American student Jon Titus. At first, he found it difficult to generate much interest in his machine, but after he demonstrated it to the publishers of *Radio-Electronics* magazine, they agreed to feature it in their July 1974 issue. The Mark-8 was advertised as a DIY (Do-It-Yourself) project. Titus supplied the microprocessor on a circuit board, but users had to buy all the other electronics and parts separately.

THE FIRST APPLE

The Apple 1 home computer looks primitive today, but when it was launched in 1976, it was a breakthrough in many ways. For one thing, these Apple computers were sold as complete circuit boards, which needed only a screen and keyboard to be added. Many users built their own cases for the Apple 1 and connected cassette players to store programs. The computers could also be programmed in BASIC, a computer language that was much more like English than the machine codes that earlier home computers used.

Connector for TV display

Wooden case added by user

Cutout title was a personal touch added by this Apple's owner

Power connector

Clip held display monitor

Keyboard added by user

Major companies at Silicon Valley:

1. YouTube
2. Oracle
3. Facebook
4. Mozilla
5. Google
6. Hewlett Packard
7. Yahoo
8. AMD
9. Asus
10. Intel
11. Nvidia
12. Adobe
13. eBay
14. Apple Inc.
15. Symantec
16. Quantum Corporation
17. Applied Materials Inc.
18. Seagate Technology
19. SanDisk
20. National Semiconductor
☆ Stanford University

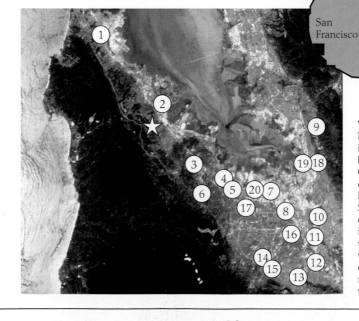

San Francisco

United States of America

VALLEY OF COMPUTERS

Many of the world's largest computer and information technology (IT) companies are based in a single valley near San Francisco, California. New technology has been developed here since the late 19th century, largely due to the work of researchers at Stanford University. Since the 1970s, many computer pioneers have worked here, including Steve Wozniak and Steve Jobs, who started the company called Apple Inc., which was one of many that began making computers. At that time people gave it the name Silicon Valley, after the silicon that went into making computers' microchips.

TINY GEARS

MicroElectroMechanical Systems (MEMS) are micromachines built on silicon chips and are usually less than 0.04 in (1 mm) across. They are made by the same processes used to build microprocessors and other printed circuit elements. Microscopic cogs, magnified here on a human palm, form part of some MEMS devices. These are used in the accelerometers that tell smart phones which way up they are, and in car airbags.

HAND-BUILT BY ROBOTS

This industrial robot is manufacturing circuit boards in an automated factory in Seoul, South Korea. The use of robots is essential to the production of computers today. Not only do robots build computers faster, but they also work more accurately than humans. Programmed instructions ensure that the robot places the components on the circuit boards precisely. Though very expensive to install and set up, robotic production lines are more efficient and cheaper to run than those employing human workers.

Circuit board

Robotic arm places component at the correct location

BUILDING MICROCHIPS

Microchips are physically tiny and made from materials that are chemically extemely pure. Even very small amounts of unwanted chemicals or single grains of dust can prevent them from working properly. Microchips are built in chambers called clean rooms, where the air is carefully filtered and checked to ensure it has very low levels of dust and chemical vapors. The workers wear special clothes such as coveralls, masks, and gloves to ensure they do not introduce contamination themselves.

Supercomputers

In the early years of computing, almost every machine was faster and more powerful than those that existed before. By the 1960s, people were building computers of many kinds, with characteristics that various users wanted—cheapness, compactness, reliability, or high speed. From then on, the computers that were designed for the highest possible speeds became known as supercomputers. The phrase "super computing" was coined long before the first electronic computers were made—it was first used in 1929 by the *New York World* newspaper to describe tabulating machines made by IBM for Columbia University.

SUPERCOMPUTER OR NOT?
Not every large and fast computer is a supercomputer. The people seen here are working in the control room of a IBM 360 computer (built 1964–78), which is a mainframe—one of a class of machines that many users can connect to via terminals. A mainframe can perform many operations at the same time, as demanded by its users. A supercomputer, in contrast, can handle a large amount of data to carry out a single complex mathematical task at a time.

Engineer uses an infrared viewer to search for overheating in a Cray supercomputer

SHAPED FOR SPEED
In the 1970s and 1980s, the Cray Corporation in the US built many supercomputers that were the fastest in the world at the time. Many of these were cylindrical—such as this Cray 1-S supercomputer developed in 1979—in order to reduce the lengths of the connectors between different circuits. This meant that signals traveled between the circuits as quickly as possible. It also gave Cray supercomputers an iconic appearance that has always been a part of their appeal.

TOP OF THE LEAGUE
This Cray Jaguar became the fastest supercomputer in the world in November 2009. The Cray Corporation built it for the Oak Ridge National Laboratory in the US. Scientists use it for research in many areas of science, including alternative energy, astronomy, climate change, and nuclear fusion. The Cray Jaguar has been upgraded many times since it was installed in 2005, and is now 75 times faster than it was at the start—capable of performing over 2 quadrillion calculations per second. Amazingly, it houses around 45,000 microprocessors!

Node, a PC-like device with processors and memory, runs a complete program on a chunk of data

High-speed network connection to share data if required

Chunk of data within node

Microprocessor carries out vector processing—by performing one step of a program on many chunks of data at once

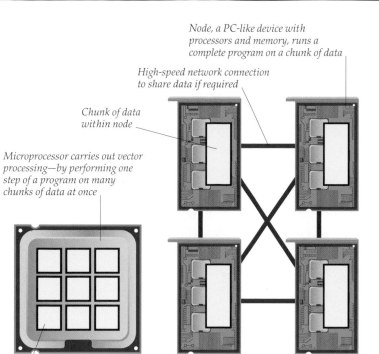

Vector processing

Distributed memory processing

Chunk of data within microprocessor

Unlike home computers, most supercomputers today are specially built for specific customers and are often designed to perform one particular task. These tasks almost always involve a great deal of number crunching—running complex mathematical calculations on enormous sets of data. Supercomputer speeds are measured in floating point operations per second (FLOPS). A floating-point operation is a simple problem with decimals. Today's supercomputers have speeds of several petaFLOPS—one petaFLOP is 1 quadrillion FLOPS.

CHECKMATE
Early valve-based computers could play chess, but it was many decades before the best software and the most advanced computers could beat the top human player. This finally happened in 1997, when the supercomputer Deep Blue defeated chess champion Gary Kasparov.

THINKING FAST
While ordinary CPUs process numbers one by one, supercomputers process data much faster by chopping up a big task into chunks of data to be processed at the same time. They usually do this in one of two ways—vector processing or distributed memory processing. Vector processors run their program on many chunks of data at once, applying each step of the program in sequence. In distributed memory processing, several PC-like machines called nodes work together on the same task, each node running a complete program on a larger chunk of data. They are coordinated via high-speed connections so that together they complete the whole task. Today, most supercomputers use distributed memory, whereas ultra-fast graphics chips use vector processing.

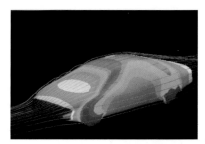

SMOOTH TRAVEL
Engineers use supercomputers to design efficient cars. The computers predict how the shapes of the cars will affect the drag caused by the air that flows over them when they move. This helps engineers to understand how to reduce drag as much as possible, in order to cut fuel consumption.

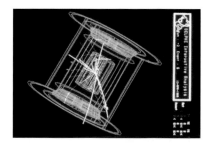

PROBING MATTER
Nuclear physicists create precise simulations inside supercomputers of how matter behaves at a scale smaller than an atom. The supercomputer calculates what happens, according to theory, when subatomic particles collide. The physicists compare this to their experiments with real particles in particle accelerators.

Software

THE "WELCOME" SCREEN THAT POPS UP when someone switches on a computer would not appear without software. Software refers to the sets of coded instructions—programs—and the data that they need. This is different from hardware, which is a computer's circuitry, casing, and the rest of its physical parts. Most people use software through a graphical user interface (GUI) with drop-down menus, windows, and a moveable pointer. The GUI acts as a visual arena where the user interacts with the computer.

OPERATING SYSTEM

The software that controls the computer's basic functions is called its operating system (OS). It is the master software, controlling how all other running software uses the processing power of the CPU and the computer's memory. It is kept in the RAM and run by the CPU whenever the computer is on. The OS also controls input and output. It interprets the meaning of the keys pressed on the keyboard and the clicks on the mouse, translating them into signals that programs can use. Since the early 1980s, operating systems have communicated with their human users through a graphical user interface (GUI). Microsoft Windows is the most widely used OS series today—the GUI here belongs to Windows 7.

Applications currently running are displayed on the screen

Task Manager application shows how CPU is being used and how busy it is

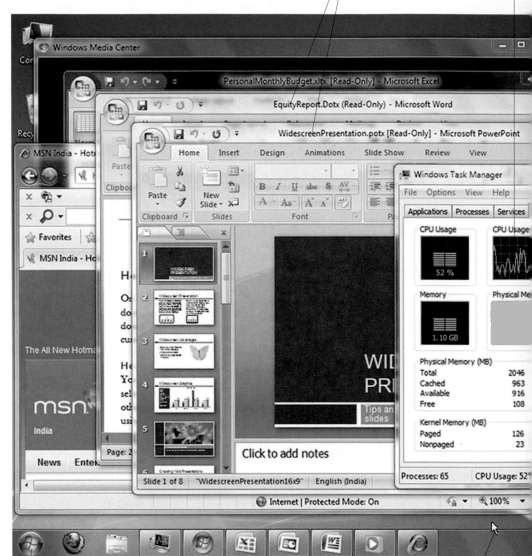

Start button gives access to a menu that lists all applications

Taskbar icon represents application that is running

Pointer is controlled by the mouse, and its position lets the user know when to click the mouse to select an option

ORGANIZING DATA

Computer users store data in blocks called files. Files are often grouped together into folders, or directories, to make finding them easier. The icon seen above represents a folder in Windows 7—the directory icon is modified to show the kinds of file it contains. Different types of files can be distinguished by the last few letters of their names—their "file extension." Extensions are used by the OS to select relevant applications to open different files. A file that ends with ".wav" or ".mp3," for instance, is a type of audio file, while ".bmp," ".jpg," or ".gif" are extensions of different image files.

Mozilla Firefox logo

SURFING THE WEB

When users need to access information on the Internet (see pages 44–45), they use programs called web browsers that allow them to search or surf the web. When accessing a web page, the browser sends a request for the page and then displays the data it receives. This is the logo of Mozilla Firefox, a web browser second only to Internet Explorer in popularity. Firefox is an example of freeware—a type of software that can be used without paying a fee. Firefox is not the original name of the browser—it was previously called Phoenix and then Firebird, but both names had already been used for other software.

OS sends processed data to the printer when required, and the printer keeps the OS informed about its progress

Printer

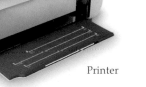

OS sends detailed instructions to the display screen to show the graphical user interface (GUI), which provides an easy way for the user to interact with the OS and other applications

Play all music

Go to Library

tworking | Users

21249
847
65
0:00:12:10
1309 / 4092

rce Monitor...

l Memory: 55%

23:34
15-12-2010

Cabinet carries the motherboard with CPU and RAM

Mouse

Movements of the mouse pointer pass directly, as input data, to the OS in the CPU

CHANGING THE PICTURE
Photo editing programs, such as Adobe Photoshop, allow users to alter images in ways that only specialists could previously achieve. Such software is not only able to improve the appearance of an image by changing its contrast or color balance, but can also apply a wide range of special effects. It is now possible to merge many pictures effortlessly to create an imaginary, but realistic, scene.

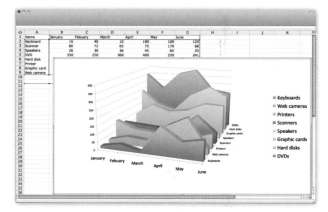

WORKING HARD
Many types of software have developed mainly for use in business. People use spreadsheet programs to store and analyze data, such as sales figures. Once a user enters figures, the program calculates statistics such as totals and averages, and displays the data in a whole range of charts—such as this 3-D chart that shows the number of items of different products sold each month. Students commonly use programs such as word processors and presentation software for their schoolwork.

MEDIA CENTERS
Users often run programs such as iTunes and Winamp to play music—mainly of the compressed ".mp3" file type. To be useful, a media player has to be able to run many video file types, including high-definition (HD) video, which is of high quality and highly compressed—to save space. Many of these programs allow users to purchase and download audio and video content from stores on the Internet.

Media application playing a movie

SECURING YOUR SYSTEM
Computers, especially those connected to the Internet, are vulnerable to a wide range of security threats, including viruses and worms (see page 49). Special software is essential to protect computers, the data they contain, and their users. Firewalls and antivirus programs (see page 51) help users defend themselves against computer-borne threats.

Programming

PUNCH CARDS
In 1801, the French inventor Joseph Marie Jacquard invented a loom that could weave finely patterned cloth automatically—and do it much more quickly than by hand. Although this loom was not a computer, people could program it using punch cards. These were long strips of cardboard filled with holes that corresponded to the threads making up each pattern. In the 1950s and 1960s, people used punch cards in a similar way to input the programs that ran on early computers.

COMPUTERS EXIST TO RUN PROGRAMS. A program is a series of instructions that tells a computer what to do next. In a simple program, a task is broken down into its most basic steps. The computer doesn't understand what links each step and just follows the instructions. A more complex program is divided into sections called subroutines. Each one performs a smaller part of the program, can be used many times, and exchanges data with other subroutines. This makes the program smaller and easier to understand. Programmers write their programs in one of many specialized computer languages, which they call "code." Regardless of the programming language, a computer converts, or compiles, the program into machine code—a string of numbers that microprocessors recognize. Some programmers write snippets of code and store them in libraries on the Internet. Others use these fragments to build their own programs easily, without having to start from scratch each time.

PROGRAMMING LANGUAGES
Programmers, or software engineers, write their instructions using a programming language. Several languages are used, each one suited to a different purpose. The BASIC language was made to be simple enough to use on personal computers. PHP helps program websites, while C++ helps write large programs. This snake game was written in a language called Java, which allows programmers to write code that works on almost any kind of computer.

THE FIRST PROGRAMMER
In the 1840s, Lady Ada Lovelace, the daughter of the English poet Lord Byron, worked with Charles Babbage, the inventor of some early mechanical computers (see page 7). She created a program on punch cards for one of Babbage's machines, the Analytical Engine. This complicated machine was never built and the program was not used. Nevertheless, Ada Lovelace is regarded as the first computer programmer. In 1979, the US military named a new programming language Ada in her honor.

A TURTLE'S DESIGNS
In the 1980s, small robots—called turtles—were used to teach the type of very precise instructions needed in programming. The robots drew patterns on the floor according to their program and could make this spiral by following a few steps—distance equals one unit, move forward one unit, turn right, repeat steps 2 and 3, distance equals 2 units, and so on. Programs could apply the same technique on a screen to make a line graphic.

Turtle robot

Pattern created

A snake in a game programmed in Java

An Ariane 5 rocket launches into space

ROCKETING TO DISASTER
A badly designed program can cause a disaster. The European Space Agency uses Ariane 5 rockets to launch spacecraft. In 1996, an Ariane 5 rocket exploded on its first test flight. The guidance program was written for an older rocket and did not work with the Ariane 5 rocket's new launch system. Spacecraft often run using old-fashioned computer systems, because engineers are confident their programs do the job well and making a new one is risky and expensive. NASA's Space Shuttles used a computer designed in the 1970s with less processing power than most mobile phones!

THE MILLENNIUM BUG
Programs need to be cleared of mistakes. However, bugs, or errors, still get through. As the year 2000 approached, experts found an error that came to be called the Millennium Bug. Old programs recorded a year as just two numbers—1999 was 99, and the following year would be 00. So there was a possibility that the world's computers would record year 00 as 1900 not 2000, causing computers to stop working properly—or at all! Programmers worked hard to beat the bug by making computers record a year as four numbers. When 2000 rolled in, no major problems were found.

Icon representing Millennium Bug

KNOWING WHEN TO STOP
This robot has been programmed to wash cups. It looks for and sees the cup, moves its arm to it, picks it up, turns on the faucet, and starts washing the cup. However, the program must also include a final step that tells the robot to put the cup down—and not wash it again. Without this end command, the robot would keep washing the same cup forever.

Computer-generated imagery

COMPUTER GRAPHICS HAVE DEVELOPED RAPIDLY since the 1980s, transforming the world of visual effects in computer games and films. Before computer-generated imagery (CGI), games were just rows of text, sometimes with very primitive graphics based on a few characters. Thanks to CGI, computer games now include graphics that are almost lifelike, and films rely on CGI to create highly detailed digital models of creatures and places that look amazingly real. CGI is also widely used in other industries, such as architecture, publishing, and engineering. Creating and manipulating images needs fast computers, a lot of memory, and sophisticated display systems.

BEFORE CGI
This animator is using his own reflection to provide the right expression for his drawing of a character from the animated film *The Lion King*. Until CGI was developed, animators had to hand-draw characters many times, with slight differences between each version. When photographed and played back in quick succession, the sequence of images would look like a single moving image.

Basic grid made of geometric shapes

Character is illuminated

Each dot helps in creating a facial map for accurately recording expressions on the computer

Texture makes the character more lifelike

Reflective marker forms part of a series that specifies the body's position

Blue color of bodysuit makes it easy to digitally remove the actor later, leaving the map of his body

Glove maps the details of the fingers

VIRTUALLY REAL
A CGI character—such as Master Chief from the *Halo* series of video games—takes shape in stages. In the first stage, an artist defines the 3-D outline of the character using a mesh of lines. Next, the artist overlays a surface on this mesh and adds a source of light, creating shadows. In the final stage, he or she builds up full details of color and texture. Once created, the character can be viewed from different angles and made to move—without the need to redraw it.

Architects discussing CGI design of buildings

BUILDING IN AIR
CGI has revolutionized the way architects work. Rather than producing hand-drawn artworks, they can now create graphics that can be easily modified at the touch of a button and viewed from any direction. Once the overall layout and dimensions are agreed upon, the architects can add colors, textures, and other details. Sending CGI files to colleagues via email is easier and faster than sending paper drawings through the mail.

FROM REAL TO REEL
Actor Andy Serkis was transformed into a creature named Gollum in *The Lord of the Rings* movie trilogy using CGI motion-capture technology. Serkis wore a special suit while enacting his role. Special cameras and software captured details of his shape and movements. Artists then created the CGI figure of Gollum. This existed in a 3-D form inside the computer's memory, the 3-D positions of Gollum's body parts corresponding to Serkis's. Gollum was animated by making him mimic Serkis's movements.

Gollum's face is animated with expressions from the actor's face

Limb length matches that of the actor

Fingers and other extremities are extended

FILMS WITHOUT PEOPLE
Toy Story, released in 1995, was the first full-length feature movie to be made entirely using CGI. The filmmakers chose to use toys as characters because they are fairly easy to model and animate—CGI technology at the time was not adequate for creating human characters. This was partly because human bodies are complex and partly because everyone is familiar with how people look and move, so imperfections in human CGI characters are easy to spot.

Buzz Lightyear, a character from *Toy Story*

A VIRTUAL WORLD
Tron was the first movie to make extensive use of CGI technology. Although not very successful when it was released in 1982, *Tron* led to the use of CGI in many other films. In many of its scenes, human actors were added to CGI backgrounds. The CGI light cycles—or digital motor cycles—seen here were created for the movie, in which human players explore a virtual world of computer games. As they move, these cycles leave behind colored walls of light, which they must then avoid. Video games were also released based on *Tron*. A sequel, *Tron: Legacy*—featuring far more advanced CGI—was released in 2010.

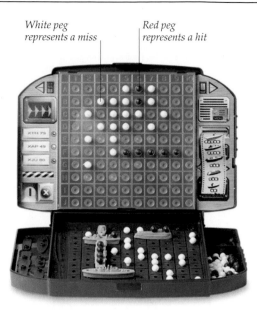

White peg represents a miss

Red peg represents a hit

Games and consoles

THE COMPUTER GAMES INDUSTRY IS HUGE, earning more money than movies. People from around the world can play against each other via the Internet. Some online games involve thousands of players in a virtual world. A staggering 12 million people play the *World of Warcraft* game alone! Games and programs have one thing in common—they both follow a set of rules. So it is not surprising that some of the earliest programs helped re-create simple games on a computer. By the 1970s, video game machines were among the first computers to be popular in homes. Powerful microchips have enhanced gaming, making games very lifelike.

ATTACK AND SINK
An early use of computers was to enhance popular board games, such as chess and *Battleship*. Players could play a game of chess against a computer by entering their moves on a simple keypad. Invented in the early 1900s, *Battleship*—seen here in a board version—was originally played with just pencil and paper. However, by the 1970s, a computerized version had added sounds and lights to the game. Text-based games, such as *Colossal Cave Adventure*, were common in the early days of gaming. Since they didn't need graphics, they were easier to program.

PONG
Video games started to become popular in the 1970s. The first games were very simple because most computers could store only tiny programs. One of the most successful early games was *Pong*. Two players using joysticks moved a paddle up and down on a screen to bounce a ball into their opponent's goal. This game was first played on coin-operated arcade computers, but by 1975, engineers developed a console that plugged into an ordinary television.

Stick control bends in all directions to move an item on screen

NOT JUST CHILD'S PLAY
In 1977, the Atari 2600 console changed the way video games could be played. Instead of having a single game programmed into it, the Atari 2600 played a variety of games stored on interchangeable plug-in cartridges. Players could use one machine to play several games, such as *Breakout* and *Blackjack*. They could play alone or with another player. By the 1980s, video gaming had even become a sport. The best video game players—many of whom were children—competed in tournaments to become world champions. These events even attracted the attention of top sportsmen of the day, such as Ron Cey, a 1980s baseball star—seen here watching a game of *Asteroids* at an Atari tournament.

Xbox 360 controller

PAC-MAN

Early video games were inspired by the real world in their graphics. However, by the 1980s, many games had little connection with the real world. The most popular was *Pac-Man*, developed in Japan in 1980. The Pac-Man character had to eat all the dots set out inside a maze, while avoiding being touched by ghostlike enemies. Pac-Man was so popular that it soon became more than a game, with a cartoon series and Pac-Man clothes and toys.

Pac-Man
eating dots

Player can race the
others or play alone

Button can control
other functions for a
game character, such as
crouching or jumping

AT THE ARCADE

In the 1980s, the best place to play video games was in an arcade. Games arcades were not a new idea, but by this time, mechanical games such as skittles and pinball had been largely replaced by coin-operated video games. Arcade machines can be much bigger than a home console, and many are designed to make the game experience as real as possible. This racing game, for example, has controls similar to a real car.

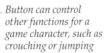

ALL ABOUT CONTROL

The most exciting video games are played on consoles. A console's computing power beats that of most personal computers today. That processing power is used to create detailed graphics and high-speed action. Early consoles were played with a paddle (wheeled controller) or a joystick. Modern console controllers allow players to perform several functions at once. They can also be equipped with a pack that makes them judder, or vibrate, adding a new dimension to the game.

PLAYING ON THE MOVE

Handheld gaming machines have been around since the early days of computer gaming. They became popular because they gave users the freedom to play video games anywhere. In the 1990s, the Nintendo Gameboy became the first really successful handheld console, loading different games from cartridges. Modern portable consoles, such as the Sony PlayStation Portable (PSP)—shown above—are equipped with wireless technology, so players can connect to games playing in computers nearby, as well as download music and videos.

EXERGAMING

Since the start of computer gaming, parents have complained that their children spent too long sitting in front of video game screens, instead of being more active. The invention of exergaming has combined the benefits of exercise with the fun of gaming. Exergaming needed a new type of controller, as the players used their whole bodies to control the game. In *Dance Dance Revolution*, released in 1998, players danced on a pad to music. Other exergames use handheld controllers that detect motion, and players can use these like a bat or racket.

Each area of dance pad, or stage, is sensitive to pressure

Controller used in *Guitar Hero*

ADDING A NEW DIMENSION

The Mario character has been appearing in video games since 1981, when he was the hero of the *Donkey Kong* games. To begin with, Mario appeared as a 2-D graphic, known as a sprite, moving left and right along flat platforms. In 1996, Mario went 3-D, and could travel in all directions. The rapidly increasing processing power of graphics microchips allowed the extra mathematical calculations needed for creating 3-D games. This was the advance in technology that marked a big step forward in the way games looked and were programmed. In a 3-D game, every item on screen is a 3-D object, and whenever a character in the game moves around, its shadow shifts.

An inflatable model shows off the latest 3-D Mario figure

MORE THAN A GAME

In the 1980s, video games were often based on movies. *Star Wars*, *E.T.*, and the *Indiana Jones* films all gave rise to games, and by the 1990s, video games and films were often created at the same time. As video games became more popular, filmmakers began making films based on them. *Super Mario Bros.*, the first of these movies, was released in 1993. Later, Sonic the hedgehog appeared in an animated film and Lara Croft inspired two movies based on the *Tomb Raider* series. In 2010, the film *Prince of Persia: Sands of Time* re-created several scenarios—such as the swordfight shown above—from the long-running *Prince of Persia* game series, which dates back to 1989.

GUITAR HEROES

Most video games are designed to work with a console's normal controller. However, some of the latest releases use specific controllers to make the most of a game. In 2005, players of *Guitar Hero* got to be rock stars by strumming along to songs on a guitar-shaped controller. The *Karaoke Revolution* game, released in 2009, provides microphone controllers for players to sing into. The player's score reflects how close their singing voice is to the correct melody.

LOOK, NO HANDS!

Players using 2011's gaming machines are no longer connected by wires to the console, leaving them free to move around the room as they play. Some machines have handheld wireless motion detectors that send commands to the console through radio signals. The Kinect system developed by Microsoft for the Xbox 360 console does away with controllers entirely. Instead, cameras capture the movements of players, putting their gestures into action on the screen.

ALMOST THE REAL THING

Lionel Messi, Argentina's soccer star, looks amazingly real in this *Pro Evolution Soccer 2011* game. Gaming machines have a microchip—the GPU (graphics processing unit)—that is dedicated to producing, or rendering, graphics on the screen. Images and graphics in a computer game are made of little patches of color animated in 3-D in a virtual world in the console's memory. Modern GPUs can render hundreds of millions of these patches in real time, making today's video games more lifelike than ever.

Networks

NETWORKS CONNECT COMPUTERS TOGETHER, helping them share data or other resources. The computers can be linked to each other, and to other devices, such as printers. This can be done either by wires or fibers—forming a wired network—or wirelessly, using radio signals. Local area networks (LANs), which can be wired or wireless, cover small areas and are used within schools, offices, and other public places. LANs can be connected to each other over wide area networks (WANs). The number of networked computers and other devices is steadily growing, and so is the amount of data they share with each other. It is our insatiable hunger for bandwidth—the capacity to transfer data—that drives the quest for better technology.

WHY NETWORK?
Computers are networked partly so that people can use them as communication devices, sending not only text-based messages to each other, but images, audio files, and videos, too. Networking also allows computers to work together—in this office, for instance—by sharing data, software, and processing power, and by accessing other devices, such as projectors and scanners. Networked computers are less likely to lose data, since it can easily be copied between machines.

Fiber is made of flexible strand of glass

TYPES OF NETWORK
There are two main ways to connect computers together so that resources such as files and applications can be shared—peer-to-peer and client-server connections. In a peer-to-peer network, each computer shares all or part of its resources, and all the computers on the network have equal importance. Client-server networks have a central computer—the server—that manages resources such as storage space and web access on the network and sends data to other computers—clients.

Server

Client

Peer

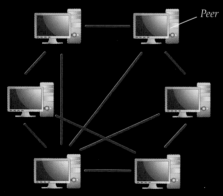

1 PEER-TO-PEER
Most computers come loaded with the software needed to set up a peer-to-peer network. Each computer is known as a peer. These networks are prone to being hacked because the peers only handle their own security and not that of the network. Peer-to-peer networks can also be slow because each peer handles requests from the user as well as from other peers.

2 CLIENT–SERVER
In a client-server network, the server controls security and distributes software upgrades across the network, so the users of the client computers do not need to worry about these things. This makes these networks more secure. Client–server networks are often faster, and it is usually easier to add new computers to them. However, servers can be expensive and complex to maintain.

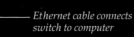
Ethernet cable connects switch to computer

WIRED NETWORKS

In many schools and offices, the computers that make up a LAN are connected together by wires. Devices called hubs, switches, or routers connect computers into wired networks. Usually, such wired networks use the ethernet system, in which packets of data, called frames, are exchanged. Each frame has a data header that identifies its starting point and destination on the network.

WIRELESS NETWORKS

In a wireless network, radio waves link computers together. Devices called wireless routers send and receive the radio waves. People often use wireless LANs, or WLANs, in homes and public places, such as cafés, airport lounges, or even parks. Though WLANs are much more convenient than wired networks, they are less reliable and less secure—radio waves can suffer interference from electrical equipment and can be intercepted by anyone with the right software on their wireless laptop. One popular wireless technology is called Wi-Fi—a special wireless communication system that allows devices to connect to each other and provides Internet access.

MOVING QUICKLY

Some wireless networking systems are designed to work over short distances. TransferJet is one such technology—it makes use of radio waves and has a range of only a couple of inches. Simply touching two TransferJet-enabled devices together triggers a transfer of data between them. Each device can identify other devices nearby that are enabled and users can set them up to transfer only to and from selected devices. For example, placing this digital camera on top of this media storage device transfers the contents of the camera to the device at a very high speed.

Data being sent via Bluetooth

Data being received

PATHWAYS OF LIGHT

Optical fibers are used in many long-distance computer networks. Light travels down the fibers over great distances—this is possible because it travels down the core of an optical fiber by constantly bouncing off the sides of the fiber, using a principle called total internal reflection. Light transmits all kinds of data as short flashes arranged in coded patterns. Undersea bundles of fibers can transfer as much as 100 gigabits of data per second (see page 47). In many cases, optical fibers have replaced metal wires, because they are unaffected by electrical interference and the data signals can typically travel 60 miles (100 km) before fading.

LET'S SHARE

These cell phones are sharing data via Bluetooth. This is another short-range wireless networking technology designed to work between devices of different types. Bluetooth technology uses frequency-hopping, a system in which the radio frequency used to send data changes rapidly. Frequency-hopping signals are less affected by radio interference and also do not interfere with signals sent by other systems.

The Internet

A **COMPUTER ON A NETWORK** relies on a direct connection to a central server or to other networked computers in order to transfer data. When a connection snaps, communication within the network is affected. In the 1960s, the US government realized that its computer network was vulnerable to attack—a few disconnections could prevent the network from functioning, which could be a serious problem during wartime. The solution to this problem was an internetwork—a network of networks that eventually became known as the Internet. If one connection was broken, data could travel via another route. This internetwork ran according to a set of rules—the same ones that ensure the smooth flow of data on the Internet today.

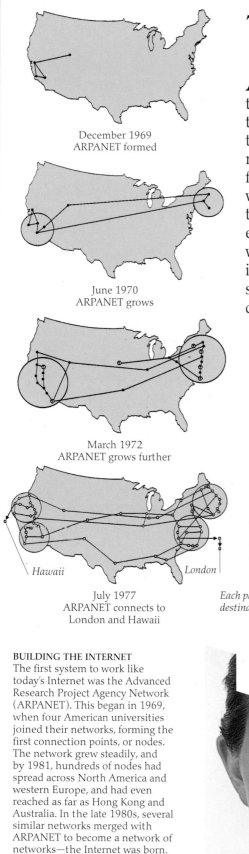

December 1969
ARPANET formed

June 1970
ARPANET grows

March 1972
ARPANET grows further

Hawaii   *London*

July 1977
ARPANET connects to
London and Hawaii

BREAK IT UP AND BUILD IT UP
A computer sends data through the Internet in small bundles, or packets. Each packet has an address showing where it is headed and hops along many Internet servers, down miles of cable, until it reaches its destination. The data packets from one dataset, such as from a photo, do not have to travel the same route, or even arrive in the correct order. Once all the packets arrive at the destination computer, it reassembles them into their original form.

Different packets, indicated by the colors, take different routes to the destination

Each packet contains destination address

BUILDING THE INTERNET
The first system to work like today's Internet was the Advanced Research Project Agency Network (ARPANET). This began in 1969, when four American universities joined their networks, forming the first connection points, or nodes. The network grew steadily, and by 1981, hundreds of nodes had spread across North America and western Europe, and had even reached as far as Hong Kong and Australia. In the late 1980s, several similar networks merged with ARPANET to become a network of networks—the Internet was born.

As it is sent, image is broken up into chunks of data

Data set sent

44

SERVING A PURPOSE
Servers are the information warehouses of the Internet. These specialized computers store data, such as emails and web pages, which can be accessed by other computers and devices, or clients (see page 42), connected to the Internet. Key servers of the Internet handle so much traffic that they require server farms—thousands of individual servers working together. Servers are usually kept in a secure and separate room. They need a cool environment, since all the computers working together can get very hot.

Optical fiber made of glass

Polyethylene covering protects cable

Stranded metal wire provides strength to cable

Petroleum jelly acts as waterproof cover for optical fibers

Undersea Internet cable

DATA CONNECTIONS
The Internet employs a range of connection types. Many homes are connected through copper telephone lines or television cables. Cell phones and laptops receive Internet traffic over wireless radio links. Optical fibers carry data along the Internet's "backbones"—thick cables that connect nodes and even run over the seabed. A single cable carries hundreds of high-speed optical fibers bundled together, each see-through fiber carrying data in the form of flickering laser light.

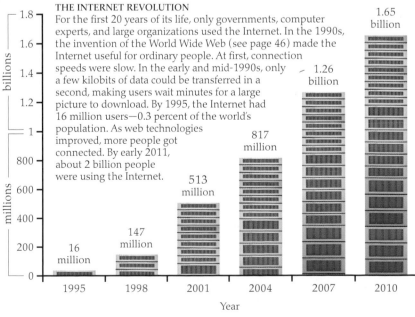

Image reconstructed at receiver's end

Traffic route unused by data is shown in white

Packet coding indicates where it belongs in original image file

All packets arrive at the same point

Data set received

Internet server on the traffic route used by data is shown in color

THE INTERNET REVOLUTION
For the first 20 years of its life, only governments, computer experts, and large organizations used the Internet. In the 1990s, the invention of the World Wide Web (see page 46) made the Internet useful for ordinary people. At first, connection speeds were slow. In the early and mid-1990s, only a few kilobits of data could be transferred in a second, making users wait minutes for a large picture to download. By 1995, the Internet had 16 million users—0.3 percent of the world's population. As web technologies improved, more people got connected. By early 2011, about 2 billion people were using the Internet.

Internet users

billions | millions

1.8
1.6
1.4
1.2
1
800
600
400
200
0

16 million — 1995
147 million — 1998
513 million — 2001
817 million — 2004
1.26 billion — 2007
1.65 billion — 2010

Year

Connecting the world

To MANY PEOPLE, THE INTERNET and the World Wide Web (WWW) are the same thing. However, the Internet is the physical network that spans the globe—including the actual cables and computers, and the set of rules that allows data to flow seamlessly. One of the first applications of the Internet was the Bulletin Board System that began in the 1970s, letting users leave messages for each other on public computers, and eventually gave rise to chatrooms. Another was the file transfer protocol (FTP) system for exchanging large files. And of course, the Internet now carries millions of emails every day. Most people connect to the Internet to access the web, an ever-growing collection of interconnected pages, carrying a mix of text, images, and videos.

FATHER OF THE WEB
The British scientist Tim Berners-Lee invented the World Wide Web (WWW) in 1989 as a way of sharing data. His system allowed users to view information on other computers, so a web-enabled computer could access far more data than could be stored in it. Berners-Lee made his invention public, and the web has since changed the world dramatically.

Random fragment of text pulled from the WWW

http is one of the rules that control web data transfer

LISTENING TO THE WWW
Web traffic surging through the Internet contains fragments of text and images. Each little piece means something to someone, but when put together, it is just a mixture of raw data. *The Listening Post* display at the Science Museum in London, England, pulls random strings of text from chatrooms—places on the web where people can have conversations with one another—and flashes them on a series of screens. The displayed fragments of text are often meaningless, but occasionally something readable appears. This art installation highlights the millions of interactions that occur on the web and shows how the Internet has connected people unlike anything before.

Google

Eyewitness Computer

SEARCH

SEARCHING THE WEB
As the number of web pages grew, it became harder to find information of interest. Search engines were developed to pinpoint the right web pages. Early engines used web crawlers—software that reads text on a web page and indexes it, before moving to the next one. Modern search engines, such as Google, still use web crawlers to find pages, and also complex mathematics to highlight the ones that might be most suitable in response to a particular search.

SHARING RESOURCES
The Internet can be used to share data and resources in many ways. Scientific research programs need powerful computers to perform complex calculations to help solve problems quickly. The Einstein@Home project uses the Internet to harness the power of computers volunteered by users. When the machines are not being used, Einstein@Home runs a program on them, using their spare capacity to process data collected by astronomers searching for pulsars—small superdense stars that spin around hundreds of times in a second. The program displays a spherical map of the sky—as seen on the right—with known pulsars shown in magenta. On August 12, 2010, the Einstein@Home system announced a previously unknown pulsar.

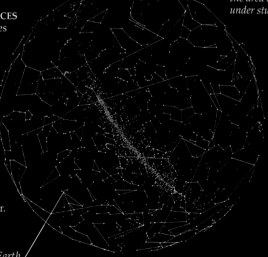

Marker indicates the area of the sky under study

Diagram of sky shows constellations of stars visible from different parts of Earth

WEB ADDRESSES

Every web page has a unique address called its URL, or uniform resource locator. Web pages are delivered from servers to browsers using a set of rules called the hypertext transfer protocol (http), so a web page's URL always begins with "http." The domain name comes next and often starts with "www" to show human users it is part of the world wide web. Many commercial domain names end in ".com." The domain-name part of the URL tells a computer which server it should contact to access the web page.

WWW is used in most URLs but not all

Image is a hyperlink and leads to a new page

URL of website

Name of the web page appears on top of a browser window

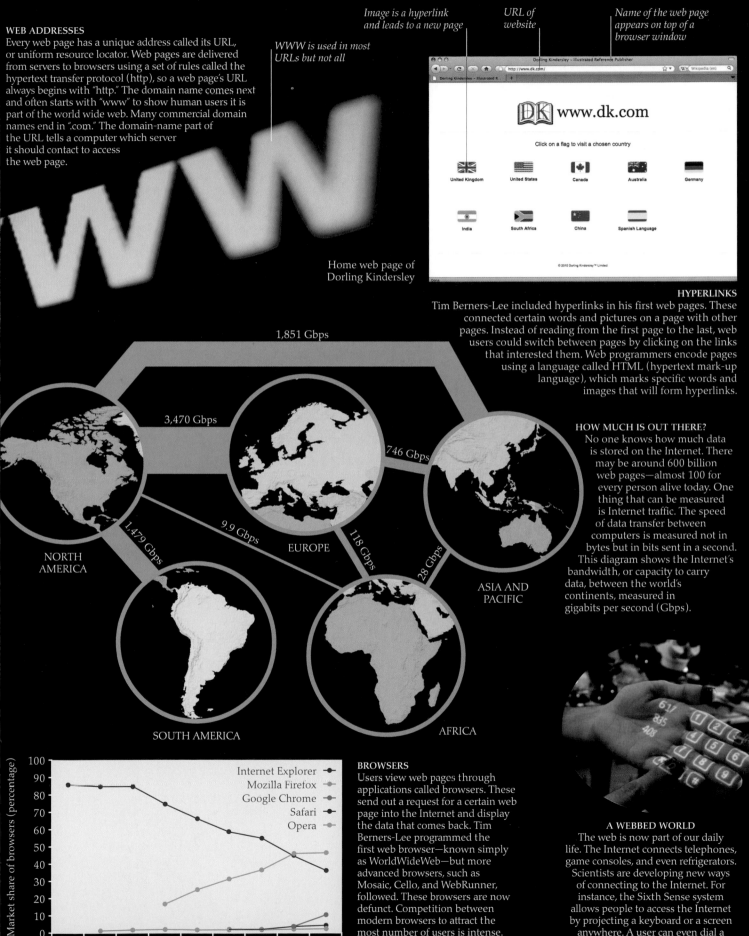

Home web page of Dorling Kindersley

HYPERLINKS

Tim Berners-Lee included hyperlinks in his first web pages. These connected certain words and pictures on a page with other pages. Instead of reading from the first page to the last, web users could switch between pages by clicking on the links that interested them. Web programmers encode pages using a language called HTML (hypertext mark-up language), which marks specific words and images that will form hyperlinks.

HOW MUCH IS OUT THERE?

No one knows how much data is stored on the Internet. There may be around 600 billion web pages—almost 100 for every person alive today. One thing that can be measured is Internet traffic. The speed of data transfer between computers is measured not in bytes but in bits sent in a second. This diagram shows the Internet's bandwidth, or capacity to carry data, between the world's continents, measured in gigabits per second (Gbps).

1,851 Gbps

3,470 Gbps

746 Gbps

NORTH AMERICA

1,479 Gbps

9.9 Gbps

EUROPE

118 Gbps

28 Gbps

ASIA AND PACIFIC

SOUTH AMERICA

AFRICA

BROWSERS

Users view web pages through applications called browsers. These send out a request for a certain web page into the Internet and display the data that comes back. Tim Berners-Lee programmed the first web browser—known simply as WorldWideWeb—but more advanced browsers, such as Mosaic, Cello, and WebRunner, followed. These browsers are now defunct. Competition between modern browsers to attract the most number of users is intense.

Internet Explorer
Mozilla Firefox
Google Chrome
Safari
Opera

Market share of browsers (percentage)

100 90 80 70 60 50 40 30 20 10 0

2002 2003 2004 2005 2006 2007 2008 2009 2010
January of each year

A WEBBED WORLD

The web is now part of our daily life. The Internet connects telephones, game consoles, and even refrigerators. Scientists are developing new ways of connecting to the Internet. For instance, the Sixth Sense system allows people to access the Internet by projecting a keyboard or a screen anywhere. A user can even dial a phone number via a keypad that is projected on the user's hand.

The wild wild net

THE INTERNET HAS CREATED A WHOLE NEW WAY for people to meet, work together, and even shop. Unfortunately, this has also allowed criminals to use the Internet for stealing and cheating. Although every computer on the Internet has an owner, no one is in charge of the entire network. This makes it tough for Internet security experts to track down hackers—people who break into other people's computer systems. The battle for law and order on the Internet is often compared to the American Wild West, with gunslingers, sheriffs, and innocent bystanders.

THE TROJAN HORSE
In Greek mythology, the Trojan Horse attack was a ploy by which Greek soldiers got past the security of the city of Troy and destroyed it. They hid inside a giant wooden horse, sent as a gift. A computer Trojan does the same thing. It appears as a type of helpful software but once installed, it allows hackers to break into and establish a connection with the user's computer to control it.

HACKING IN
One of the first hacks was done using a whistle! In the 1970s, US telephone exchanges used special tones to communicate with each other. John Draper, a computer programmer, discovered that the sound of a whistle—found in a cereal box—was like one of these tones. Blowing the whistle tricked exchanges into thinking that an ongoing call had finished, which let Draper make calls without being charged for them. Modern hacks generally involve cracking a password. Hackers run programs that try every combination of letters and numbers until they find the right one. They also use malicious software, such as spyware, to trick users into giving out passwords. However, other software, such as anti-spyware and firewalls (see page 51), helps users defend themselves against such attacks.

Megaphone boosts the sound of slogans

Music system plays slogans during protest march

COMPUTER INFECTIONS

Malware is the name given to computer viruses and worms—computer programs designed to cause problems to any user on the Internet. Computer worms do not attack an individual computer. Instead, they swarm through the Internet by making use of the way computers communicate. Worm attacks clog up the Internet, slowing traffic through the routers. On May 4, 2000, the ILOVEYOU worm, stored in this floppy disk, spread across the world, causing widespread damage. Viruses damage a computer by wiping its memory or preventing it from turning on. Unlike a worm, a virus activates only when the receiver opens it.

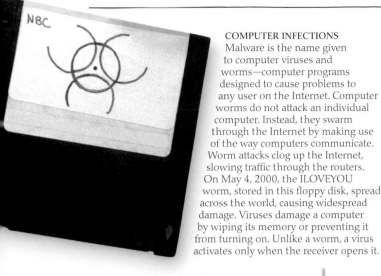

UNWANTED MESSAGES

Mailboxes in the real world can become overfilled with unwanted "junk" mail. It is free to send junk mail on the Internet, so in the digital world, users can easily receive hordes of emails and messages that are either useless or contain harmful viruses. They are collectively called spam. Spam clogs up a user's email inbox, making it hard for the user to communicate properly and preventing messages from being sent or received. Many spam emails carry links to fake websites that ask users for personal details, such as bank account numbers and passwords. This kind of fraud on the net is called phishing.

Overfilled mailbox

WATCHMEN OF THE NET

Not all hackers break into computer systems for personal gain. Some hackers are hired by organizations to help test the strength of security systems. Other groups of hackers are self-appointed watchmen of the Internet. They organize protest marches and design attacks against organizations that, they believe, are being unjust. Anonymous is one of these groups. It has no leaders and its members may not even know the names of one another. During public protests, members wear masks like that worn by "V"—a fictional hero who used hacking for good causes in the film *V for Vendetta*. The masks also hide their identities.

ATTACK OF THE ZOMBIES

Among the most powerful tools used by people attempting cyber-crimes are botnets, short for "robot networks." These are networks of thousands, even millions, of ordinary computers that have been hijacked by hackers, without their owners' knowledge. Botnets are used for sending out millions of spam emails in a short time. They are also used for denial-of-service (DOS) attacks, where the combined power of the botnet is used to overload Internet servers and prevent users from accessing websites.

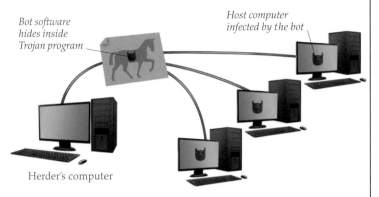

Bot software hides inside Trojan program

Host computer infected by the bot

Herder's computer

1 CREATING A BOT ARMY

The hacker who develops a botnet is called a herder. He or she gains access to computers through a Trojan horse—usually spread by spam emails. When users launch the Trojan software, they unknowingly grant access to the herder, and their computers become zombie systems under the control of the herder.

Computer sends out emails to other computers to add them into the botnet

Activate command sent by herder

Herder's computer

Zombie computers

2 THE ATTACK

The botnet's zombie computers become active only when they receive a command from the herder. The herder can also use the zombies to send infected emails to other computers, creating more botnet members. In a DOS attack, all the zombies are instructed to contact the same Internet server over and over again. This huge and sudden demand for service jams the server and it shuts down.

CYBER WARFARE

Sometimes, wars can be waged on the net. The US Cyber Command (CYBERCOM) is in charge of defending American military computers, which are under regular threat from programs designed to steal military secrets. In 2007, Estonia's web services were knocked out by huge DOS attacks from Russia—after the Estonian government decided to move a Russian war memorial. In 2010, an Internet worm called Stuxnet damaged the computers in an Iranian factory thought to be making nuclear weapons.

CYBERCOM emblem

Defense and security

A LOT OF THE INFORMATION stored on computers is private, whether it is personal documents, bank details, or government secrets. As a result, computers need to identify their correct users and keep their private files secure. The simplest identification system is the password, inherited from the watchwords used by Roman guards. Only people who knew the right watchword were allowed through. But no computer is ever completely secure. Hackers (see page 52) can exploit weaknesses in security systems, or simply steal passwords, to gain access illegally. Computer experts are creating new technologies to make user identification more accurate.

EVERYDAY ENIGMAS
Private computer files are encrypted, or transformed into unreadable codes, using a set of rules, or cipher. In World War II, the German military encrypted its messages using electromechanical devices, such as this Enigma machine. Messages were encoded with a cipher set using a series of numbered cogs, or gears. Its designers mistakenly believed that only another Enigma machine, set up using the same cipher, could decode the messages. Modern computer encryption uses mathematical ciphers that make the codes very hard to crack.

CAPTCHA IF YOU CAN
Captcha stands for "Completely Automated Public Turing test to tell Computers and Humans Apart." Users take the Captcha test to gain access to a free service, such as email. The user types in the characters shown in a picture, which is warped so that only a human can figure them out. Humans pass this test, but Captcha filters out computers using programs designed to hack into these free services—to send out spam, for instance.

Technician setting the rotors of the bombe

This rotor is one of 36 that enabled the bombe to check every possible Enigma cipher

A bombe decoder

CRACKING CODES
People can use computers to try to decode secret or private data. One of the world's earliest computers was used to decipher the Enigma codes during World War II. British mathematician Alan Turing used decoders called bombes to test all 17,576 possible Enigma ciphers until the coded messages were cracked. He also developed the idea behind Colossus, an enormous, programmable, digital code-cracker, which was built in 1943 to crack even tougher codes.

FIREWALLS

A network carries information between computers, but it must also stop unwanted traffic, such as viruses or spy programs, from getting through. This is done with a virtual barrier, called a firewall, which protects a computer system from unauthorized access. The traffic between computers passes through the firewall, which scans and filters the passing packages of data to check for damaging software.

Trusted computer allowed access through firewall

Protected computer system

Firewall

Computer access blocked by firewall

Unauthorized computer system

BODY IMAGE

Computer systems can also control access in the physical world. The shape of the face, the fingerprint patterns, and the sound of a voice are all unique to a person. Computers can use this biometric information as a security identification that is always available for checking. For example, a computer can recognize a user's face by converting its shape into a 3-D map of triangles. This can then be compared to a reference map of the user's face stored in the security system. Some measurements, such as the length of the nose and distance between the eyes, are the same even if the person is smiling or frowning—and will help the computer confirm a user's identity. Biometric security systems are an important part of secure government installations, such as nuclear power plants, missile silos, and centers for intelligence agencies.

Network of triangles follows the shape of the face in three dimensions

Graphic displayed by antivirus software to show that it is busy scanning

HEALTH CHECKS

Every computer needs a regular health check in the form of a virus scan. Antivirus software does this by checking all the files stored in the computer. It looks for patterns that might indicate viruses, worms (see page 49), or other unwanted software. Since new threats and infections are discovered every day, an antivirus program regularly downloads security updates to ensure it is always looking for the right things.

LOOK INTO YOUR EYES

Many biometric systems are still under development. The recognition systems still get it wrong too often to use on a large scale just yet. In the future, biometric security scans will be routine everywhere. One of these scans could involve a person's eyes. The patches of color in the iris around the pupil can be mapped, as can the mesh of blood vessels covering the retina at the back of the eye—both of which are unique to each individual. Even identical twins that share identical DNA and similar fingerprints can be told apart easily by such a scan. Eye scanners are already being tested at some airports.

Iris scanner

Living on the net

TODAY ALMOST ONE-THIRD OF THE PEOPLE on Earth—nearly 2 billion people—have access to the Internet. The Internet was set up to carry information between computers, but its inventors had little idea of how it would change the way that people—the computers' users—lived. These netizens, or citizens of the net, do the same things as people without access to the net. They work, learn, shop, and chat with their friends. The difference is that an online computer or phone allows them to do all this from anywhere—making it easy to chat with a friend on another continent, go to classes in their living rooms, or share their views with millions of like-minded people.

IN THE BEGINNING
The first email to employ the @ sign was sent in 1971. Ray Tomlinson invented the system to send messages to any computer connected to the infant Internet. Earlier electronic messages could not travel outside one network. The @ sign was added to indicate to which machine, or domain, an email was to be sent.

IM application window showing list of friends

Caller's face appears on the screen as she talks

TALK NOW!
Instant messaging (IM) is a way for people to communicate through a computer network in real time. This removes the need to wait for questions and answers to travel back and forth. People have been using IM for nearly 50 years. At first it worked only on computers on the same network. Today, the typed messages travel in the blink of an eye to any computer on the Internet. Users of IM applications, such as MSN and Yahoo! Messenger (left), can connect only to members on a list of friends—no one else can be a part of the conversations. Users in online chat rooms, however, can connect to any user in those chat rooms.

Emoticon helps convey a basic emotion, making the interaction more personal

WEB 2.0
Social networking websites, such as Facebook and Orkut, enable people to connect and interact with all their friends at once. Members can choose to chat privately or join in with group discussions. This way of using the net, in which every communication is channeled through one system, and the users themselves produce the contents of a site, is known as Web 2.0. A wiki is another example of a Web 2.0 service. It is an informative website that can be added to or edited by anyone.

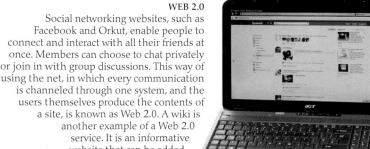

Facebook profile page

STAYING UPDATED

With so much to see and do on the Internet, netizens have to work hard to stay up to date. A number of software developers have created technology to help users stay updated. Really simple syndication (RSS) works for any site carrying this orange icon. A software called a RSS reader tracks updates on users' favorite websites—such as news services and blogs (personal, web-based logs)—and displays them for the users in the form of RSS feeds—dynamic lists that automatically update themselves with new items on the websites. Instead of having to search for interesting information, the users can simple click on what catches their eye on an RSS feed.

RSS icon

SEE YOU, SEE ME

The idea of seeing the person on the other end of the telephone has always intrigued people. Science fiction stories of the 1960s depicted video phones long before people had computers in their homes. Live video messages contain more data than a simple voice call, and it was not until the 21st century that good quality videos could be made small enough to send through the Internet quickly. It is easy to make video calls between two iPhone 4 devices, for instance, using Wi-Fi to access the Internet.

Phone's tiny camera provides a live video feed

End

Smaller video window shows what the other person is seeing

LEARNING AT A DISTANCE

Learning on your own is a difficult job. Having a teacher explain things and answer questions has always been the best way of doing it. That used to mean that people living in remote communities, far from the nearest school, had to spend a lot of time living away from home. Today, web technologies, such as video conferencing, can create a classroom wherever there is a computer. Students and teachers talk via video links, and homework is delivered by email. In the future, it might be quite normal for teachers to give classes throughout the day from across the world.

Information about a place of interest is displayed instantly

Icon indicates a place of interest on the structure

MAP / List

Jules Verne Restaurant

Eiffel Tower [324 metres]

AUGMENTED REALITY

An Internet connection does not just make activities easier, it can also augment, or enhance, them. This is especially true of mobile devices that can access the Internet, such as smartphones—which can pinpoint a user's location. Augmented reality applications pull information from elsewhere on the net and display it as layers on top of a camera image of the surroundings. For example, when tourists point their phones at a famous landmark, they can not only see extra details about it, but also—as in this case of the Eiffel Tower in Paris, France—see the best local restaurant, and even determine if any friends are nearby.

Virtual worlds

Visor has screens for each eye, to give a stereoscopic (3-D) view

FEELING EVERY BUMP
Virtual reality not only creates sights and sounds, but also responds to the user's movements. Motion detectors let people use their hands and feet in a VR world. This snowboarder is seeing a virtual course in his visor and the scene changes with every move of his head. Using his feet, he tilts the board to steer, and it wobbles with every virtual bump and jump.

Berkman Center building in Second Life

IMAGINE BEING ABLE TO EXPLORE forgotten ruins in a faraway continent, or bumping across the surface of Mars on a dune buggy. Computers today create worlds that seem incredibly real, but are part of virtual reality (VR). Virtual means "almost," and in computer terms, it refers to something that appears to be there but is created wholly by a program. Virtual reality makes games seem more lifelike and online interactions feel more real, but VR has serious uses, too. In 2007, a stomach surgeon in the US operated on a patient located thousands of miles away in Argentina! A robot made the cuts and stitches. Thanks to VR technology, the surgeon could see every detail of the patient, and control the robot through the Internet. Virtual reality may, in the future, become part of everyday life.

A VIRTUAL LIFE
Second Life is an online VR world, where anyone can set up a home, make new friends, start a business—or just fly around like a superhero. The residents of Second Life are animated characters called avatars. More than 21 million avatars have strolled around Second Life since it was created in 2003, and many real-world organizations have set up headquarters there. In 2006, the Berkman Center, a research institute that studies the Internet, invited experts to discuss virtual reality—at a meeting held in Second Life! Since 2006, Second Life's graphics have been steadily refined.

ENTER THE MATRIX
Computer-generated worlds have been explored in stories for years. In the *Tron* films (see page 37), human users travel to a digital world and battle evil programs. The *Matrix* films have taken the idea of VR several steps further. A virtual world, called the Matrix, is perceived as the real world by enslaved humans. They are just avatars, kept in order by the machines. In the movies, human rebels can hack into the Matrix and change part of its programming, bending the laws of physics according to their will—as seen here. As VR technology becomes more lifelike, there is a danger that users could lose touch with reality.

The rebel Neo (left) battles a machine agent in *The Matrix*

SIMULATORS
VR systems have been particularly useful as training simulators. Instead of using real guns, soldiers may practice with a VR system—as shown here—which teaches them to respond in the right way during combat. Pilots may also use VR cockpits to simulate those in planes for practicing what to do in emergencies that are too dangerous to re-create in real life. The cockpit rocks and rolls as the pilot steers. Another simulator even turns satellite maps of distant planets into 3-D scenes, so space scientists can explore them.

Each avatar represents a user sitting at a computer in one of a range of locations across the world

Avatar can be made to look like anything the user wants—even an alien creature

Robots

PEOPLE WERE IMAGINING MACHINES that did the work of humans as early as 2,400 years ago. However, building a working robot proved to be difficult until the arrival of computers. A robot's computer brain can be programmed to perform a simple job many times over. In the 1980s, robots began replacing human workers in industrial assembly lines. Superstrong robot arms now build car bodies much faster than a human team could. However, robots are no good at solving problems. If an instruction is not in the program, they cannot perform it. Scientists are figuring out ways of making robots more versatile—and more intelligent.

BEFORE ROBOTS
The idea that robots could lighten the workload of humans has always inspired people. In the 1890s, Canadian engineer George Moore designed Steam Man, a mechanical machine powered by a steam engine, which could walk on two legs and was strong enough to pull carts. Although undoubtedly a skillful piece of engineering, Steam Man, like other early robots, was almost completely useless because simpler machines, such as wheeled vehicles, did the same jobs better.

LEARNING TOGETHER
One way computer scientists are trying to make robots more intelligent is by getting them to compete against each other. Since 1999, robot teams have been competing in the RoboCup soccer tournament. In most of the matches, the teams are made up of identical robots, and the competition is over how well the robots are programmed to work together in ways that beat the other side. Even though the robots are only about 12 in (30 cm) tall, and move slowly, it is still exciting to see them mimic human behavior!

Camera in head allows robot to see and react to ball and goal

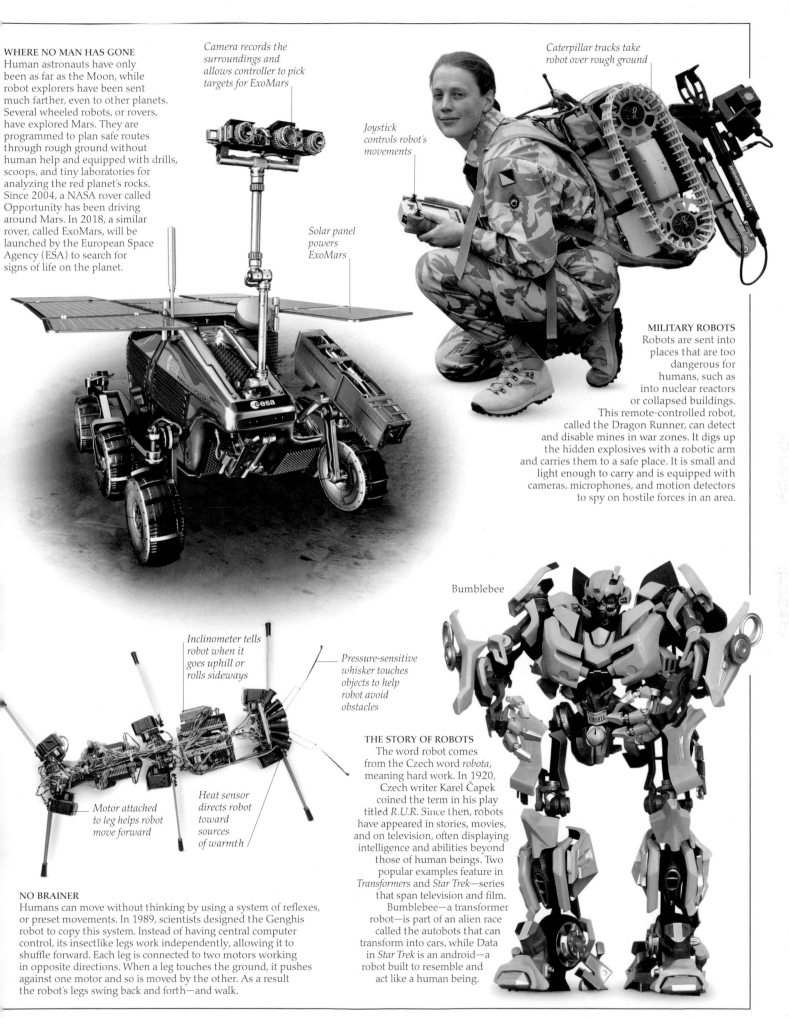

WHERE NO MAN HAS GONE

Human astronauts have only been as far as the Moon, while robot explorers have been sent much farther, even to other planets. Several wheeled robots, or rovers, have explored Mars. They are programmed to plan safe routes through rough ground without human help and equipped with drills, scoops, and tiny laboratories for analyzing the red planet's rocks. Since 2004, a NASA rover called Opportunity has been driving around Mars. In 2018, a similar rover, called ExoMars, will be launched by the European Space Agency (ESA) to search for signs of life on the planet.

Camera records the surroundings and allows controller to pick targets for ExoMars

Solar panel powers ExoMars

Caterpillar tracks take robot over rough ground

Joystick controls robot's movements

MILITARY ROBOTS

Robots are sent into places that are too dangerous for humans, such as into nuclear reactors or collapsed buildings. This remote-controlled robot, called the Dragon Runner, can detect and disable mines in war zones. It digs up the hidden explosives with a robotic arm and carries them to a safe place. It is small and light enough to carry and is equipped with cameras, microphones, and motion detectors to spy on hostile forces in an area.

Inclinometer tells robot when it goes uphill or rolls sideways

Pressure-sensitive whisker touches objects to help robot avoid obstacles

Motor attached to leg helps robot move forward

Heat sensor directs robot toward sources of warmth

Bumblebee

THE STORY OF ROBOTS

The word robot comes from the Czech word *robota*, meaning hard work. In 1920, Czech writer Karel Čapek coined the term in his play titled *R.U.R.* Since then, robots have appeared in stories, movies, and on television, often displaying intelligence and abilities beyond those of human beings. Two popular examples feature in *Transformers* and *Star Trek*—series that span television and film. Bumblebee—a transformer robot—is part of an alien race called the autobots that can transform into cars, while Data in *Star Trek* is an android—a robot built to resemble and act like a human being.

NO BRAINER

Humans can move without thinking by using a system of reflexes, or preset movements. In 1989, scientists designed the Genghis robot to copy this system. Instead of having central computer control, its insectlike legs work independently, allowing it to shuffle forward. Each leg is connected to two motors working in opposite directions. When a leg touches the ground, it pushes against one motor and so is moved by the other. As a result the robot's legs swing back and forth—and walk.

Stronger and better

THERE IS HARDLY ANY AREA of human health that cannot be improved by computerized devices. They help the visually impaired to see, replace lost limbs, help organs work properly, and can even enhance strength. But advanced computers alone are not enough. Strong, lightweight materials are needed, too, and for many applications, accurate and efficient motors. The science of bionics deals with the implantation of computerized devices into the body, but robotics also plays a part by providing mechanical caregivers, nurses, and even surgeons.

Flesh-colored prosthetic arm

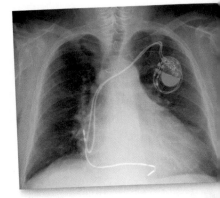

A STEADY BEAT
First used in 1958, pacemakers are implanted electronic devices that supply regular pulses of electricity to the heart, correcting the irregular rhythms of damaged hearts. Modern pacemakers contain microchips that can track the heartbeat and automatically adjust the pulses sent to the heart during activities such as exercise or heavy lifting. Doctors can use radio links to adjust pacemakers from outside the body if needed.

A HELPING ARM
The most advanced artificial limbs contain microchips that can be controlled by the user's brain. This baseball player's nerves are connected to the wires of the artificial limb, allowing him to give instructions directly with his brain to throw the ball. Sensors in the hand send feedback about position and pressure to the brain through the nerves, helping the user judge how hard his artificial hand is gripping the ball.

Camera tracks moving objects

COMPUTERS THAT CARE
In many parts of the world, the number of elderly people is rapidly increasing and many of them need to be cared for. There is an increased demand for caregivers, which is not being met. But computerized assistance is now at hand—robots, such as the Rollin' Justin shown here, can perform very simple household tasks or help people move around their homes. They can also provide company, as pets do. However, replacing human helpers with robots also means that elderly people will become more isolated from society than they already are. Robots are not a great substitute for human friendship.

Finger is closely modeled on human finger

Headrest

Computer screen displays lists of words that are selected by Hawking and spoken by speech synthesizer

SEEING WITH A NEW EYE

The retina lines the back of the eye, and its function is to convert the light that enters through the pupil into tiny electrical signals. These signals travel along the optic nerve to the brain—allowing us to see. When damage or disease interferes with this process, microchips can sometimes be implanted inside the eye. Rather than changing light to electricity, these artificial retinas receive signals from external cameras, which are then used to trigger impulses in the optic nerve. To the user, it seems as if the camera input is coming from the eye itself.

Artificial retina connected to optic nerve

Footrest

Motor moves joint to precise angles

ENABLING PEOPLE

The British scientist Stephen Hawking, who has almost no control of his body and cannot speak, is able to work and communicate thanks to technology. A sensor translates tiny movements of his cheek into electrical signals that control a speech synthesizer—a device that generates an artificial voice. Although improved synthesizers have since been developed, Hawking has decided not to upgrade his, because he feels its voice is now his own.

Soft-ended clamp allows for a gentle grip

SUPER STRENGTH

Computerized machines can do more than replace lost human functions. Exoskeletons, such as this prototype, combine the enormous strength of machines with the delicacy and fine control of human limbs. Users simply move their hands and arms as they usually do, and computerized sensors in the exoskeleton detect these actions, making the exoskeleton move in the same way via a series of rods and motors. There are many areas where exoskeletons could be used, such as rescue operations where heavy—yet precise—lifting is required.

HEARING COLOR

People with impaired senses can enhance their remaining senses with computerized help. In the eyeborg, electronic sensors in the device detect different colors and their patterns, each image triggering a distinct sound. By learning which sound is associated with which image, visually impaired users can recognize the objects and scenes around them. Using the device requires no surgery—the user just wears a simple head-mounted holder. Artist Neil Harbinsson uses the eyeborg to create sound paintings of places and people.

Artificial intelligence

Reply from human

Reply from computer

IMAGINE A WORLD WHERE MACHINES have replaced human workers. Computer-controlled robots do take the place of people today in some fields, lifting heavy car components or defusing bombs. However, most of them follow a strict program or require human supervision. They are not intelligent enough to think for themselves. Machines that have artificial intelligence (AI) are programmed to learn to do just that. Some AI programs use complex mathematics to solve problems that do not have a single answer, while AI toys can learn words and repeat them. However, no computer brain can yet match the intelligence of the human brain, which works in more flexible ways than today's most advanced computers. Scientists are not even sure how the human brain thinks, so AI programmers are constantly having to find new ways of building smart machines.

THE TURING TEST
In 1950, Alan Turing suggested a simple test to check a computer's intelligence. The test compares an AI computer with a human. Both are in separate rooms, while a second human—the interrogator—asks questions from a third room. If the interrogator cannot distinguish between the human and the computer on the basis of the answers, the machine has passed the test. No computer has yet fooled a human interrogator.

Multirobot formed by connected robots moves as one unit

Obstacle that needs to be crossed

SWARM INTELLIGENCE
Since computers have not yet matched human brain power, scientists are exploring other forms of intelligence. The Symbrion project consists of a swarm of tiny robots that can connect together. The robots know and remember each other's locations, constantly learning how to arrange themselves into larger structures to move around obstacles. Tackling this task together indicates a basic form of what is called "swarm intelligence."

Wheel helps robot move

EVIL AI
AI computers feature heavily in science fiction, very often in the role of a villain. In the *Terminator* movies, the AI system Skynet views humanity as a threat and creates an army of robots called terminators—such as the one shown on the left—to destroy all humans. This idea of a machine that can think and feel for itself is fascinating, yet frightening. If science can, one day, create an AI machine like this, then will people be able to control it?

Neuron from middle layer performs computation

Input neuron feeds in face data

Output neuron reports "male" or "female" face

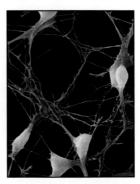

Network of neurons   Artificial neural network

AN ARTIFICIAL BRAIN
A type of AI software called an artificial neural network (ANN) mimics how the human brain uses its brain cells, or neurons, to learn. To train an ANN, programmers give it lots of examples of a task, such as distinguishing between male and female faces, but also tell it the answer to each one. It learns the rules to tell faces apart by adjusting the settings in its middle layer of artificial "neurons" to get the right answer. Then it can apply what it has learned to identify the gender of new faces by itself.

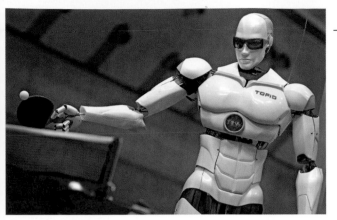

ROBOT CHAMPION

One day the TOPIO robot might be a professional ping-pong player, beating human opponents. Its Vietnamese designers have given it a body that can twist and swing in 39 different ways and eyes that can follow fast-moving balls. However, Topio still needs to practice like a human sportsperson. Its AI program remembers every ball bounce and paddle swing and uses the data to learn how to play better.

AI OR NOT?

The idea of a machine that can think is not a new one, and there are many examples of machines that have at least appeared intelligent. The Mechanical Turk, built in 1770, amazed the world by appearing to be able to play—and beat—people at chess. However, in the 1820s, it was revealed that the Turk was a hoax—although an ingenious one. A human player was hidden in the box, controlling the Turk's movements.

The Mechanical Turk

Motor for left eye

Motor for right eye

LEARNING LIKE A HUMAN

Cog was a robot built in the 1990s at the Massachusetts Institute of Technology (MIT). Cog was programmed to sense the world in the same way as humans. Scientists hoped that this would allow Cog to learn about things much like a small child does. This robot was built to look like a human, with a head and arms, making it easier for people to interact with it. Cog could turn its head toward sounds, look at objects with its camera eyes, and pick them up with its touch-sensitive hands. By showing Cog a ball and saying the word "ball," scientists could teach it to recognize a ball. This wasn't remarkable in itself, but an AI machine that began to learn in this way could perhaps one day match human intelligence.

Head swivels on neck and can look up and down

Camera helps eye to focus on objects

Finger senses pressure when touching object

Torso frame

Mechanical hand can grasp objects

Tomorrow's computers

Moving objects by thought, becoming invisible, or building robots too small to be spotted by the human eye, are ideas that have fascinated science fiction writers. However, scientists today are developing computers that will soon make these ideas a reality. Computers are becoming smaller, yet more powerful. Researchers believe that some future computers may calculate using light, not electricity, inside their CPU. Others may be controlled by brain waves, and yet others may even think for themselves! Once the benefits of new technologies are well established, consumers will demand them. This will encourage companies to develop them further, making them cheaper in the process—helping to change our lives.

Raised eyebrow mimics human expression of surprise

Ear movement indicates surprise

Jaw movement can mimic a human jaw when speaking

Eye moves to look at person the robot focuses on

Nanobot head contains sensors to detect disease-causing organism

ROBO SEE, ROBO DO

This robotic face can't speak, but it can still communicate. It uses facial expressions instead, just like humans do, and it can respond to human faces, too. Nonverbal interaction can be much better and quicker than using words for communicating feelings, since many feelings share the same facial expressions in different languages and cultures. Kismet, as this system is called, can also analyze the tones of human voices and work out which emotions may lie behind them. Technology like this may help build robots that can learn to communicate with people without the need to be programmed.

Arm ends in grappling device to hold microorganism

Microorganism

AT MY FINGERTIPS

"Augmented reality" technology—which adds layers of information on top of objects in the real world—could change the way computers provide information. In spatial augmented reality (SAR) displays, such as the mock-up display shown on the left, a camera would track a user's movements, feeding the data into a computer. This would work out what the user is pointing to—in this case, the sky bridge of the Petronas Towers in Kuala Lumpur, Malaysia. The system would then project information about the feature on to the window.

NANOBOTS

A nanobot is a tiny robot, much too small to see. Nanobots could be produced to perform medical tasks inside the body, such as destroying cancer cells and ridding the bloodstream of dangerous bacteria. They could also be programmed to self-replicate, producing trillions that could break down massive oil spills at the sea. We already have the technology to build machines only 0.00004 in (0.001 mm) across, though so far they are simply collections of gears.

REINVENTING THE TAPE

Computers are storing ever more data as their tasks become more demanding. Digital tape, used for decades, has huge storage capacity, but it is inconvenient because of the need to wind and unwind. Optical tape could be the answer. This tiny roll stores 10 GB, but it is transparent, so a laser can reach deep into it—by changing its depth of focus—to store or retrieve data from any part of the tape. The laser writes data by changing the optical properties of minute portions, or units, of the tape, modifying the way the units bend light.

Laser writing optical data onto adhesive tape

Model of imaginary nanobot

Gear movement controls nanobot arms

Switch to change intensity of light in different rooms

Icons allow access to different gadgets in a particular part of house

HELPFUL HOMES

Building robots to look after our homes is a very challenging task. An alternative approach is to build homes that look after themselves instead, using "smart" functions. Smart homes could be made of self-cleaning materials, such as glass that repels dirt. Walls could show exterior views or distant landscapes, or work as TV screens. These homes would be full of devices that could be run by a universal controller such as this one.

Fan levitates ball in *Mindflex* toy

MIND OVER MATTER

Thoughts are electrical impulses in the brain, some of which can be detected by sensors placed on the scalp. By working out the electrical patterns associated with particular thoughts, the brain could be used to control different gadgets—such as running a motor-controlled fan to levitate a ball, as shown above. So far, it is not possible to "read" thoughts, but levels of brain activity and parts of the brain associated with certain types of mental processes can be worked out. So, for instance, to switch on a device, the user might have to imagine a bright light rather than the phrase "switch on."

HIDING IN PLAIN SIGHT

Computer-controlled smart clothes will one day be able to react to the surrounding temperature, keeping the wearer warm or cool, and also change color or pattern on command. By equipping such clothes with a set of cameras, they could also be made to display a real-time image of the scene behind the wearer—the effect would be to make the wearer transparent—as in the case of this prototype jacket. If the clothing covered the head and hands, too, the wearer would become invisible—almost.

History of computing

COMPUTERS HAVE DEVELOPED IN WAYS that their inventors could never have anticipated and have become numerous and widespread in just a few decades. The Internet is the largest network of computers and has connected people unlike anything before. Computers have transformed the lives of users all over the world—in the way we can work, share knowledge, communicate, and even play, using a growing array of powerful consoles and lifelike games.

The Internet

The urge to connect with people over long distances, quickly and in the cheapest way possible, has led to many great inventions. These include the international network of computers called the Internet, and the system it runs—the world wide web.

Engineer Vannevar Bush

1945 MEMEX
Vannevar Bush proposes MEMEX—a system to record documents on tiny photographs for locating them quickly—an idea that influences the web.

1940   1950

Computers

The idea of a computer, and many of the key inventions required to build one, were developed long before the first computers were built in the 1940s. Since then, computers have advanced rapidly, becoming very popular in the process.

Prototype of Difference Engine

1822 DIFFERENCE ENGINE
Babbage designs the Difference Engine—a mechanical calculator. He extends his ideas to propose the Analytical Engine, which would have been the first computer, had it been built.

Vacuum tube

1886 TABULATING MACHINE
Hollerith's tabulating machine reads punch cards automatically. Its technology will be used to input data into many early computers.

1800   1810   1820   1830   1880   1890

1801 JACQUARD'S LOOM
Joseph Marie Jacquard's loom uses punch cards that define the patterns it weaves, making it the first programmable device. People will later use punch cards as input devices for computers.

Jacquard's loom

Hollerith's tabulating machine

1950   1960   1970

1951 WHIRLWIND
The Whirlwind computer is developed as a flight simulator. It is the first computer with an interactive video display.

1962 SPACEWAR!
Spacewar! is released but not patented. It is widely copied and influences many later computer games.

1972 PONG LAUNCHED
Pong, an electronic version of ping-pong (table tennis) goes on sale. It is the first computer game to enjoy wide popularity.

Space Invaders

Gaming

Chess was one of the first games that early computers could play. Users of the time would have been amazed at the vast range and enormous popularity of computer games now available. Dedicated gaming devices called consoles now have the processing power necessary to run fast, detailed 3-D graphics.

Pong

1978 SPACE INVADERS
Space Invaders is launched. It quickly becomes popular in video game arcades.

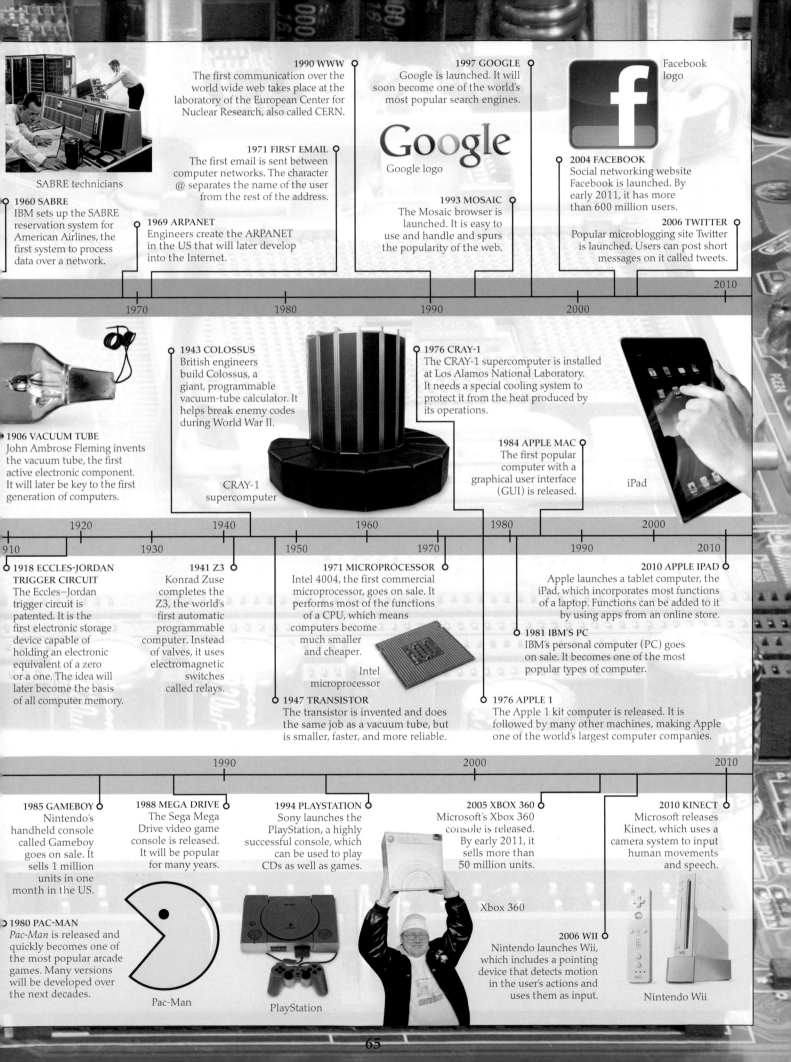

1990 WWW
The first communication over the world wide web takes place at the laboratory of the European Center for Nuclear Research, also called CERN.

1997 GOOGLE
Google is launched. It will soon become one of the world's most popular search engines.

Facebook logo

1971 FIRST EMAIL
The first email is sent between computer networks. The character @ separates the name of the user from the rest of the address.

Google
Google logo

2004 FACEBOOK
Social networking website Facebook is launched. By early 2011, it has more than 600 million users.

SABRE technicians

1960 SABRE
IBM sets up the SABRE reservation system for American Airlines, the first system to process data over a network.

1969 ARPANET
Engineers create the ARPANET in the US that will later develop into the Internet.

1993 MOSAIC
The Mosaic browser is launched. It is easy to use and handle and spurs the popularity of the web.

2006 TWITTER
Popular microblogging site Twitter is launched. Users can post short messages on it called tweets.

2010

1970   1980   1990   2000

1943 COLOSSUS
British engineers build Colossus, a giant, programmable vacuum-tube calculator. It helps break enemy codes during World War II.

1976 CRAY-1
The CRAY-1 supercomputer is installed at Los Alamos National Laboratory. It needs a special cooling system to protect it from the heat produced by its operations.

1906 VACUUM TUBE
John Ambrose Fleming invents the vacuum tube, the first active electronic component. It will later be key to the first generation of computers.

CRAY-1 supercomputer

1984 APPLE MAC
The first popular computer with a graphical user interface (GUI) is released.

iPad

1920   1940   1960   1980   2000

1910   1930   1950   1970   1990   2010

1918 ECCLES-JORDAN TRIGGER CIRCUIT
The Eccles–Jordan trigger circuit is patented. It is the first electronic storage device capable of holding an electronic equivalent of a zero or a one. The idea will later become the basis of all computer memory.

1941 Z3
Konrad Zuse completes the Z3, the world's first automatic programmable computer. Instead of valves, it uses electromagnetic switches called relays.

1971 MICROPROCESSOR
Intel 4004, the first commercial microprocessor, goes on sale. It performs most of the functions of a CPU, which means computers become much smaller and cheaper.

Intel microprocessor

2010 APPLE IPAD
Apple launches a tablet computer, the iPad, which incorporates most functions of a laptop. Functions can be added to it by using apps from an online store.

1981 IBM'S PC
IBM's personal computer (PC) goes on sale. It becomes one of the most popular types of computer.

1947 TRANSISTOR
The transistor is invented and does the same job as a vacuum tube, but is smaller, faster, and more reliable.

1976 APPLE 1
The Apple 1 kit computer is released. It is followed by many other machines, making Apple one of the world's largest computer companies.

1990   2000   2010

1985 GAMEBOY
Nintendo's handheld console called Gameboy goes on sale. It sells 1 million units in one month in the US.

1988 MEGA DRIVE
The Sega Mega Drive video game console is released. It will be popular for many years.

1994 PLAYSTATION
Sony launches the PlayStation, a highly successful console, which can be used to play CDs as well as games.

2005 XBOX 360
Microsoft's Xbox 360 console is released. By early 2011, it sells more than 50 million units.

2010 KINECT
Microsoft releases Kinect, which uses a camera system to input human movements and speech.

Xbox 360

1980 PAC-MAN
Pac-Man is released and quickly becomes one of the most popular arcade games. Many versions will be developed over the next decades.

Pac-Man

PlayStation

2006 WII
Nintendo launches Wii, which includes a pointing device that detects motion in the user's actions and uses them as input.

Nintendo Wii

Computers in numbers

THE WORLD OF COMPUTERS IS ALL ABOUT large numbers. There are over 1 billion personal computers in the world, and each one can hold the same amount of information as thousands of books and transfer it to other computers at a rate of several books per second. Over the years, the number and power of computers has grown rapidly—there are more than 100 times as many personal computers in 2011 as there were in 1971.

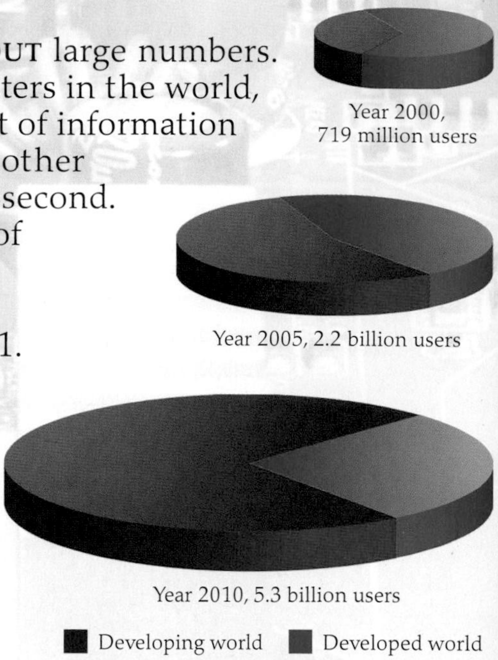

Year 2000, 719 million users
Year 2005, 2.2 billion users
Year 2010, 5.3 billion users
Developing world
Developed world

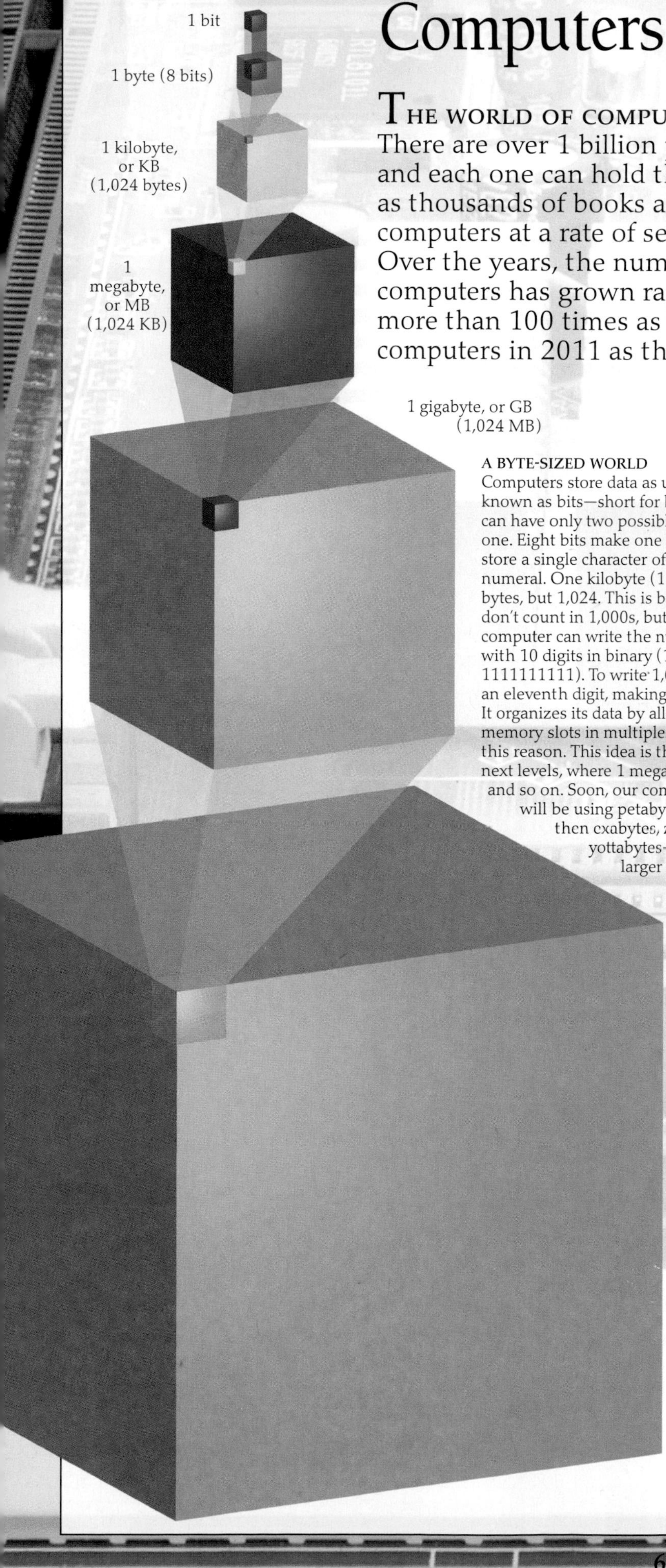

1 bit
1 byte (8 bits)
1 kilobyte, or KB (1,024 bytes)
1 megabyte, or MB (1,024 KB)
1 gigabyte, or GB (1,024 MB)
1 terabyte, or TB (1,024 GB)

A BYTE-SIZED WORLD
Computers store data as units of information known as bits—short for binary digits. A bit can have only two possible values—zero or one. Eight bits make one byte, which can store a single character of text or a single numeral. One kilobyte (1 KB) is not 1,000 bytes, but 1,024. This is because computers don't count in 1,000s, but in binary. A computer can write the numbers 0–1,023 with 10 digits in binary (1,023 in binary is 1111111111). To write 1,024, it would need an eleventh digit, making 10000000000. It organizes its data by allocating data to memory slots in multiples of 1,024 for this reason. This idea is the same at the next levels, where 1 megabyte is 1,024 KB, and so on. Soon, our computer applications will be using petabytes (or 1,024 PB), then exabytes, zettabytes, and yottabytes—each 1,024 times larger than the last.

HELLO WORLD
Although it took them several years to catch on, cell phones have grown rapidly in popularity over the last few decades. Initially, the largest growth was in the developed world. In recent years, the maximum growth in the use of cell phones has been seen in the developing world. Here, the population is growing faster, and setting-up mobile connections is much cheaper than constructing land-based networks.

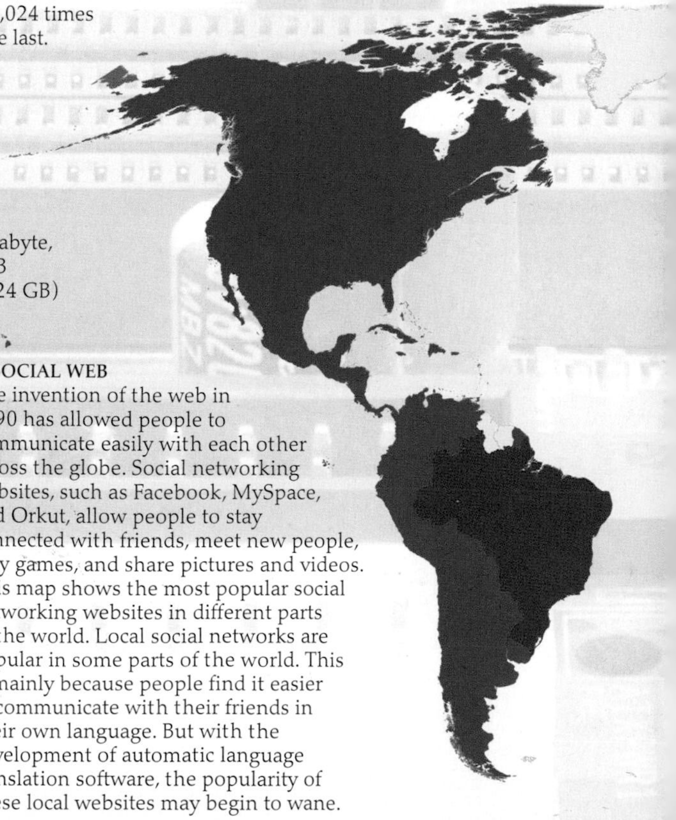

A SOCIAL WEB
The invention of the web in 1990 has allowed people to communicate easily with each other across the globe. Social networking websites, such as Facebook, MySpace, and Orkut, allow people to stay connected with friends, meet new people, play games, and share pictures and videos. This map shows the most popular social networking websites in different parts of the world. Local social networks are popular in some parts of the world. This is mainly because people find it easier to communicate with their friends in their own language. But with the development of automatic language translation software, the popularity of these local websites may begin to wane.

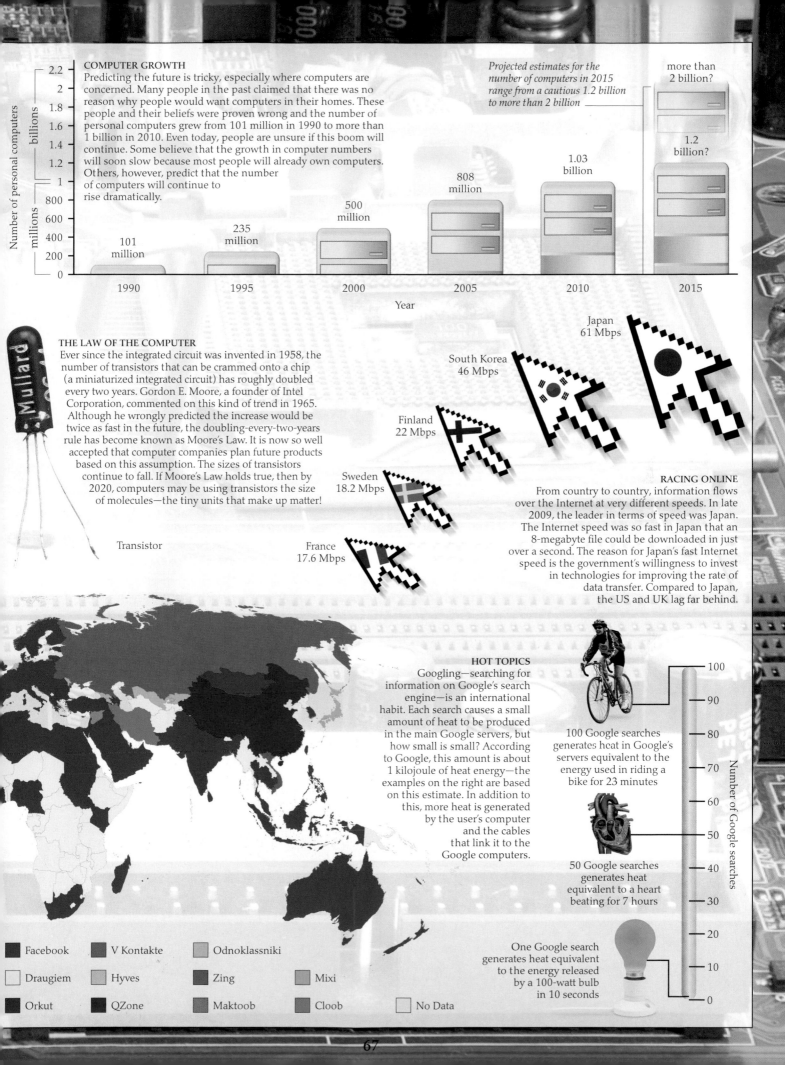

COMPUTER GROWTH

Predicting the future is tricky, especially where computers are concerned. Many people in the past claimed that there was no reason why people would want computers in their homes. These people and their beliefs were proven wrong and the number of personal computers grew from 101 million in 1990 to more than 1 billion in 2010. Even today, people are unsure if this boom will continue. Some believe that the growth in computer numbers will soon slow because most people will already own computers. Others, however, predict that the number of computers will continue to rise dramatically.

Projected estimates for the number of computers in 2015 range from a cautious 1.2 billion to more than 2 billion

more than 2 billion?

1.2 billion?

101 million — 235 million — 500 million — 808 million — 1.03 billion

Number of personal computers (billions / millions)

Year: 1990 1995 2000 2005 2010 2015

THE LAW OF THE COMPUTER

Ever since the integrated circuit was invented in 1958, the number of transistors that can be crammed onto a chip (a miniaturized integrated circuit) has roughly doubled every two years. Gordon E. Moore, a founder of Intel Corporation, commented on this kind of trend in 1965. Although he wrongly predicted the increase would be twice as fast in the future, the doubling-every-two-years rule has become known as Moore's Law. It is now so well accepted that computer companies plan future products based on this assumption. The sizes of transistors continue to fall. If Moore's Law holds true, then by 2020, computers may be using transistors the size of molecules—the tiny units that make up matter!

Transistor

Japan 61 Mbps

South Korea 46 Mbps

Finland 22 Mbps

Sweden 18.2 Mbps

France 17.6 Mbps

RACING ONLINE

From country to country, information flows over the Internet at very different speeds. In late 2009, the leader in terms of speed was Japan. The Internet speed was so fast in Japan that an 8-megabyte file could be downloaded in just over a second. The reason for Japan's fast Internet speed is the government's willingness to invest in technologies for improving the rate of data transfer. Compared to Japan, the US and UK lag far behind.

HOT TOPICS

Googling—searching for information on Google's search engine—is an international habit. Each search causes a small amount of heat to be produced in the main Google servers, but how small is small? According to Google, this amount is about 1 kilojoule of heat energy—the examples on the right are based on this estimate. In addition to this, more heat is generated by the user's computer and the cables that link it to the Google computers.

100 Google searches generates heat in Google's servers equivalent to the energy used in riding a bike for 23 minutes

50 Google searches generates heat equivalent to a heart beating for 7 hours

One Google search generates heat equivalent to the energy released by a 100-watt bulb in 10 seconds

Number of Google searches: 100 90 80 70 60 50 40 30 20 10 0

Facebook   V Kontakte   Odnoklassniki

Draugiem   Hyves   Zing   Mixi

Orkut   QZone   Maktoob   Cloob   No Data

Glossary

3-D
Having three dimensions (length, height, and depth), either in the real world, or in the virtual world of computer models or graphics.

ABACUS
An ancient calculating device that represents numbers using movable beads on a series of levels. Each level usually contains nine beads.

Bluetooth headset for cell phone

ALGORITHM
A set of rules that divides a problem into simple steps and is represented as mathematical code.

ANALOG
A device is analog if it receives input on a continuous scale, instead of the two-state 1s and 0s of digital inputs.

APP
Short for application and referring to a small program that runs on a handheld device, such as a cell phone, or a website.

APPLICATION
A program with a user interface (a display for interacting with a system), designed to perform a set of useful functions. Familiar applications include word processors and media-playing software.

CGI recreation of prehistoric flying reptile

ARTIFICIAL INTELLIGENCE
Computer intelligence created by programs that allow computers to make decisions and learn on their own.

ARTIFICIAL NEURAL NETWORK
A computer program that is set up to learn how to respond to input in a way similar to how the brain cells, or neurons, work.

AVATAR
The graphical representation of a human user in a virtual environment, such as a forum, chat room, or virtual-reality world. The word is derived from the ancient Sanskrit word for incarnation.

BINARY
A number system, also known as base two, that uses only 0s and 1s. The binary code used by computers relates to the "on" and "off" positions of electronic switches in a microprocessor.

BIT
Short for binary digit, bit stands for one digit in a computer code. Early computers accepted a 4-bit code, with just four binary digits in each line. Modern computer processors are 64-bit and can handle 64-digit codes.

BLOG
Short for web log, referring to a diary or personal accounts published on the web.

BLUETOOTH
A short-range radio system that connects computers, telephones, and many other devices.

BOTNET
A network of many computers, connected through the Internet, which is under the control of one person, who is often a hacker, called a herder.

Digital camera

BROWSER
An application used to view the contents of the world wide web. The browser sends out requests for web pages to Internet servers, which locate the files and send them back to the browser.

BUG
A mistake in a program that stops it from working or makes it work incorrectly.

CALCULATOR
A machine that performs mathematical calculations.

CGI
Short for computer-generated imagery, CGI refers to the special visual effects used in gaming and movies, among other applications.

CLIENT-SERVER
A way of setting up a network that uses central computers (servers) to manage traffic over the network and store files. Files and applications are then distributed to client computers—the ones people use—on request.

COMPUTER
A device that can receive and store information and give a response when required, while following a program—a set of instructions.

COMPUTER VIRUS
A piece of malicious software, or malware, designed to copy and distribute itself to many computers. In the process, the virus may attack or damage a computer's memory or software.

CPU
Short for central processing unit, CPU is the component that carries out computer programs and controls the responses of all the other components, such as the display screen, memory, and networking systems.

CYBER-CRIME
A criminal act committed using computers. Many cyber-crimes involve stealing information by breaking into private computer files.

CYBER WARFARE
Use of hacking techniques to overwhelm, confuse, or trick the computer networks of an enemy, stopping them from communicating effectively.

DATUM (plural, DATA)
A piece of information that has been recorded because it is useful to know.

DATABASE
A computer file that contains a collection of data. Databases are arranged so that their entries can be crosschecked, compared, and adjusted either all at once, or in specific groups.

DEBUG
To test a program in order to find and fix its mistakes, or bugs.

DIGITAL
A system that breaks down every number or command into binary code, made of 1s and 0s. Digital information is used to control the two-state switches within computers, turning them "on" or "off." A switch can be in only one of these two states.

DIGITAL CAMERA
A camera that picks up an image using a digital light sensor. The sensor converts the image into a digital file, which can be re-created on a screen or printed.

DIRECTORY
A system used to organize the way computers store files. Also known as folders, a directory may contain one or more files, or several more directories.

Flash drive

DISPLAY
The screen output device of a computer. It is often called a monitor.

DISTRIBUTED MEMORY PROCESSING
A type of data processing used by supercomputers in which many nodes (PC-like devices with their own memory and microprocessors) work together on the same task, breaking it up into large chunks on which entire programs are run to process the data.

DRIVER
Short for device driver, this is a small program that allows a computer's main programs, such as a word processor, to send commands to devices connected to the computer, such as printers.

EMAIL
Short for electronic mail, email is a message system that sends text, pictures, and small files between computers through the Internet. Email addresses include the recipient's name and their address on the Internet.

EMBEDDED COMPUTER
A computer that controls a device such as a television, car engine, or dishwasher. It is programmed to perform specific functions and is not generally accessible to the person using the device.

ENCRYPTION
A method to encode a message using a set of rules called a cipher. Without the details of the cipher, decoding a message would take a long time.

ETHERNET
A computer networking system in which computers are joined together by cables. Ethernet connections are used in local area networks (LANs) where several computers in the same area are joined together.

FILE
A package of digital information that can be opened, viewed, and edited by a program.

FIREWALL
A software barrier that stops unwanted programs and users from accessing a private computer network.

FIRMWARE
The small programs that control the functions of computer components, such as hard drives, and other computerized devices such as cell phones and remote controls.

FLASH DRIVE
Removable data storage or computer memory device that stores data on a microchip using electronic components, instead of on a magnetized hard disk drive. Plug-in flash drives, or memory sticks, are an easy way of moving data. Flash memory is also used in cameras, game memory cards, and some laptops and media players.

FLOPS
Short for floating point operations per second, a way of measuring a computer's speed. A "floating point operation" (FLOP) is a common type of calculation.

GEAR
A system of interlocking wheels that transmits spinning motion from one to the other. Gear wheels of different sizes alter the speed and power of the motion. In a mechanical computer, a small movement of one wheel is converted into a larger movement in another.

GPS
Short for global positioning system, GPS is a navigation network that picks up signals from a number of satellites to pinpoint the position of a person using a device that can access GPS.

GRAPHIC
Any image, but often referring to a computer-generated one.

GUI
Short for graphical user interface, GUI allows a user to interact with a computer by displaying buttons and windows on a computer screen that are opened, closed, or moved using a mouse or touchscreen technology.

High-definition display on LCD screen

HACKER
Someone who uses trickery or specialized software to break into another person's computer system without their consent.

HARD DISK
A type of memory store in a computer. Data is stored on the disk as patterns of magnetized or demagnetized units. It is hard compared to removable "floppy" disks once used to store data.

HARDWARE
The physical components of a computer, such as the CPU and hard disk drive.

HIGH-DEFINITION DISPLAY
A display screen made up of a very large number of pixels, producing clear and sharp images. This kind of display has a very high resolution and quality.

HYPERTEXT
A section of text linked to other documents relating to that subject. Hypertext links are used in web pages on the world wide web. Clicking on one takes the user to a related page.

INPUT
Any information that enters a computer via a device, such as a mouse, keyboard, microphone, or image scanner.

INSTANT MESSAGING
A messaging system in which users connect to each other through the Internet and share typed messages, videos, or images almost instantly.

System of gear wheels

INTEGRATED CIRCUIT
A small electronic circuit made of an assembly of elements, made from a single piece of semiconducting material, such as silicon.

IRIS
The circular muscle that surrounds an eye's pupil. It opens and closes to control the amount of light entering the eye. A computer can record the pattern of a person's iris, using it for identifying the user.

JOYSTICK
A control device used by gamers. Joysticks move back and forth and from side to side, and have a series of buttons for controlling features of the game.

LAN
Short for local area network, LAN is a computer network that connects computers and other devices in a limited geographical area.

LASER
A light source containing light waves having only one wavelength, or a combination of a few. Lasers reflect in very precise ways and can read data from optical disks, such as CDs and DVDs.

Joystick

LCD
Short for liquid crystal display, LCD is a high-quality screen that creates images by electrifying liquid crystals. Electric currents alter the color of these substances, and images are created from dozens of LCD dots, or pixels.

LOGIC GATE
An electronic switch that works according to a mathematical function. The gate may transmit, block, or redirect an electric current, or flow of data, depending upon the conditions.

MAGNETIC TAPE
A plastic tape coated in a layer of iron particles, which can be magnetized in a pattern to store information.

MAINFRAME
A central computer that stores data as well as programs, and can be used by many people at one time, via terminals, each with a keyboard and display. Mainframes are very powerful and are generally used by large organizations. Mainframes can carry out many simple tasks simultaneously.

MEMORY
Any number of systems, such as RAM or hard disk drives, which computers use to store information, such as programs and files.

MICROCHIP
A computer circuit made from a single piece, generally a wafer, or chip, of a semiconductor, such as silicon; also known as "chip." A microchip is a miniaturized integrated circuit.

MICROWAVES
Waves of radiation with longer wavelengths than infrared radiation and light waves. Microwaves are so named because they are a group of radio waves with short wavelengths. They are used in many communication systems, such as Bluetooth, Wi-Fi, and cell phones.

MOTHERBOARD
The main circuit board of a computer containing the CPU and RAM.

MP3 PLAYER
A handheld music player that stores songs and other audio files in a compressed digital format known as MP3.

MULTIMEDIA
A collection of different forms of communication that are combined into one document, such as a web page with words, pictures, and sounds.

NETWORK
A set of computers connected to each other so they can share their contents and applications, as well as processing power.

OPERATING SYSTEM
The main program that manages a computer's hardware, software, and stored files.

OUTPUT
Processed data that is given out by a computer through devices, such as display screens, speakers, and printers.

PACKET
A small section of a computer file. Files are split into packets so they can be sent through the Internet. Each packet has an address showing where it is going, where it came from, and where it fits with all the other packets, so they can be reassembled into the original file once they all arrive.

PERIPHERAL
A device that is connected to a computer. Peripherals include webcams and printers.

PERSONAL COMPUTER
A computer designed to be used by one person. It is small enough to sit on a desk and is generally used in homes and offices.

Microchip

PIXEL
The basic unit of an image. It refers to the data stored in an image file or the point on a computer display that is turned on or off to produce the image.

PROGRAM
A series of instructions that a computer follows to perform a certain task.

PROTOTYPE
The first working version of a device or a machine. Prototypes are built to see if the design works as well as intended.

PUNCH CARD
A strip of cardboard covered in a pattern of holes punched through it. The pattern of holes is a simple method of storing a computer program or computer data. Punch cards were used in the early days of computing.

Robot

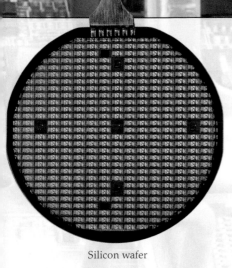

Silicon wafer

RAM
Short for random access memory, RAM is the component of the computer that stores the information being processed by the computer. This information keeps changing constantly. Information can be accessed randomly, unlike in magnetic tapes, which have to be wound to a particular point to access data.

RETINA
The light-sensitive layer at the back of an eye, which converts light into electrical impulses for the brain.

ROBOT
A machine that can be programmed to perform a set of tasks on its own without supervision.

ROUTER
A computerized device that directs files around a network. The nodes of the Internet are made up of routers, while wireless routers in homes send and receive traffic from all the computers nearby.

RSS
Short for really simple syndication, RSS is a system that monitors changes made to selected websites and displays them, so that users do not have to check them constantly for updates.

SEMICONDUCTOR
A material that can both conduct and block a flow of electric current. The electronic switches of a computer are made of semiconductors.

SILICON
The most common semiconductor, and the main ingredient in microchips and other integrated circuits. The circuits of a microchip are etched in microscopic detail on a wafer of silicon.

SIMULATOR
A computer program that re-creates an experience, such as flying a plane, as accurately as possible. Many pilots practice flying by using simulators.

SOFTWARE
A program or set of programs that provides instructions for a computer, telling it what to do and how to do it. Computer languages are used to write software.

SPAM
Unwanted emails and other messages that are sent to users' mailboxes. Spam often contains harmful files, such as viruses.

SUPERCOMPUTER
A computer that is at the forefront of computer abilities, such as processing speeds. The fastest supercomputer in 2010 was a Chinese one called Tianhe-1A.

TABLET COMPUTER
A medium-sized, handheld computer with a touchscreen operated by using a digital pen or fingertip.

THERMIONIC VALVE
A component used in computers before the invention of parts made from semiconductors. The valve used beams of electrons to block or amplify an electric current and so worked as a two-state switch.

TRANSISTOR
A piece of a semiconductor that forms part of a computer's electronic components. A transistor can let an electric current flow or block it, acting as a two-state switch in modern computers, either on its own or as part of an integrated circuit, usually on a microchip.

TROJAN
A virus or other malicious software that is hidden inside another file that appears to be harmless. Trojans can be used to create botnets.

TURING TEST
A test proposed by Alan Turing that checks whether a computer has the intelligence to match human beings.

URL
Short for uniform resource locator, URL is the unique address used by every page on the world wide web.

USB
Short for universal serial bus, a USB connection is a standard method for connecting peripheral hardware, such as a flash drive, to the main computer.

VECTOR PROCESSING
A type of data processing used by ultra-fast graphics chips in which data is broken down into many small chunks, and a program is run on them, each step of the program being applied to all the chunks simultaneously.

VOIP
Short for voice over Internet protocol, VOIP is a technology for making telephone calls through the Internet, instead of using regular telephone networks.

Thermionic valve

WAN
Short for wide area network, WAN is a computer network that covers large areas, crossing regional boundaries.

WEBCAM
A camera that feeds images or videos into a computer, or a computer network. A webcam produces video in a format that can be sent through the Internet and viewed on web browsers.

WIRELESS
Wireless refers to a connection that does not require wires. Wireless connections usually use radio waves, although some may also use infrared waves. Wireless connections can link either a computer to a network or a peripheral device, such as a mouse, to a computer.

WLAN
Short for wireless local area network, WLAN links two or more devices using a wireless distribution method such as Wi-Fi, and usually provides a connection through an access point.

WORM
A computer program that uses networks to travel through the Internet, multiplying as it goes. Worms clog up the Internet, causing it to slow down.

WWW
Short for world wide web, WWW is the main service that runs on the Internet, and is made of millions of web pages that are linked to one another by hyperlinks.

Wireless mouse

Index

Acknowledgments

Dorling Kindersley would like to thank:
Caitlin Doyle for proofreading, Helen Peters for the index, and Subhash Vohra for illustrations.

The publisher would like to thank the following for their kind permission to reproduce their photographs:

(Key: a-above; b/g-background; b-below/bottom; bl-below left; br-below right; c-center; cl-center left; cr-center right; cla-center left above; clb-center left below; cra-center right above; crb-center right below; f-far; fbl-far below left; fbr-far below right; fcl-far center left; fcr-far center right; ftl-far top left; ftr-far top right; l-left; r-right; t-top; tl-top left; tr-top right.)

akg-images: 18bl, 64crb, New Line Productions / Album / A 36br; **Alamy Images:** AF archive 7br, 37br, Ancient Art & Architecture Collection Ltd 8bl, Andia 40tr, By Ian Miles - Flashpoint Pictures 27t/5, Neil Fraser 26bl, 65cra, GIPhotoStock X 17tl, David Grossman 39tr, INTERFOTO 38cr, 61tr, 64bl, Nigel James 17cl, Jinx Photography Brands 52bc, David Lee 40-41tl, Lightly Salted 65fbr, LouisBerk.com 10cl, Adrian Lyon 52r, 53l, Dennis MacDonald 53tr, Peter Marshall 48-49bb, Mary Evans Picture Library 56tr, NetPhotos 52cl, Nordicphotos 27cl, Norebbo 53tl, Ogunn 38tl, Ian Patrick 24tl, Photos 12 60bl, Pictorial Press Ltd 2bl, 37tr, Pixellover RM 1 53br (overlaid image of iPhone), sciencephotos 71r, Roderick Smith 24ca, Jeremy Sutton-Hibbert 61tl;

The Art Archive 6br, toy Alan King 38-39b, David Wall 25r, Finnbarr Webster 65bc; **John "Pathfinder" Lester / BeCunningAndFullOfTricks.com:** 54-55b; **The Bridgeman Art Library:** Private Collection / © Look and Learn 48tl; **By HumanWare:** 21cl; "Thync Concept" - David Chacón: 63cr; **Paolo Cignoni:** 21bl; **Corbis:** Bettmann 38bl, 64tr, Roger Du Buisson 70c, Thomas Hartwell 23tr, Ed Kashi 3b, 12-13b, Patrick van Katwijk 22br, Mitsutoshi Kimura / amanaimages 42-43, Axel Koester 49tl, Kim Kulish 27t/7, Dennis Kunkel Microscopy, Inc. / Visuals Unlimited 60bc, James Leynse 45tl, Benjamin Lowy 55cr, Hank Morgan - Rainbow / Science Faction 46tl, NASA 22-23t, Charles O'Rear 65cla, Louie Psihoyos / Science Faction 5br, 57bl, Kim Kyung-Hoon / Reuters 35bl, H Armstrong Roberts 30tl, Michael Rosenfeld / Science Faction 71tl, Bob Rowan / Progressive Image 2tl, 17r, George Steinmetz 2br, 62tl, Underwood & Underwood 11c, 65tl, Randy M Ury 49cl; **Dorling Kindersley:** 8c, 26tl, 33tl, 51cr (overlaid image) 68b, Demetrio Carrasco 33tr (inset 1), Courtesy of the Imperial War Museum, London 50r, Dave King 21tr, Mike Good 68tr, Govind Mittal 20bc, 43br, Courtesy of the National Maritime Museum, London 9tr, Courtesy of The Science Museum, London 11tl, The Science Museum 8b-9b, 64cla, Clive Streeter 23br; **Dreamstime.com:** Ebelyukova 21br; **ESA:** © ESA-CNES-ARIANESPACE 35r; **Facebook, Inc:** 65tr; **Fotolia:** Sean Gladwell 44br; **Courtesy of Fuji:** 7t; **Getty Images:** 86439385 33tr (main picture), 12tl, 33bl (main picture), 39br, 56b, 57br, 65br, AFP 24bc, 31tr, 43tr, 43cr, 57tr, 59bl, 70-71bs, Bloomberg 24bl, 25tl, 27t/2, 41tr, Bob Thomas Sports Photography 69tr (inset), Buena Vista Images 20l (inset), 53br, Flip Chalfant 22l, Tony Cordoza

69tr (main picture), Coto Elizondo 33tr (inset 2), Don Farrall 69l, French School 9br, Fuse 42tl, Douglas Gibb 20-21t, Glowimages 17cb, Tom Grill 27br, Jupiterimages 58tl, Kallista Images 58tr, Lester Lefkowitz 29b, Ryan McVay 19clb, 20r, 46-47, Thomas Northcut 33clb, 68l, 71b, PIER 69b, Louie Psihoyos 36tl, Mark Segal 29tr, SSPL 7bl, 9c, 10bl, 12bl, 13tr, 16t, 27t/4, 34tl, 34bl, 64clb, Stockbyte 70l, Stocktrek 22-23c, Stephen Swintek 45br, Brian Sytnyk 62bl, Thinkstock Images 43tl, Three Images 37l, Travelpix Ltd 27cr, Vstock LLC 52br (inset), 53l (Overlaid onto mobile phone screen), WireImage 40tl; **Vicens Giménez:** 59bc; © **Google Inc. Used with permission:** 65tc; **Honda (UK):** 24-25b; **Hullie:** 11br; **Erik Klein of Vintage-Computer.com:** 28tl; **The Kobal Collection:** New Line Cinema 37bl, Walt Disney Pictures 40bl, Warner Bros 55tl; **Lenovo:** 6t; **Mattel, Inc.:** Mindflex® and associated trademarks and trade dress are owned by, and used under permission from, Mattel, Inc. © 2011 Mattel, Inc. All Rights Reserved 63bl; **Used with permission from Microsoft:** 1, 36bl; **Pranav Mistry:** Lynn Barry 47br; **Mozilla:** 2c, 32bc; **Museum of Natural Sciences, Brussels:** 8t; **NASA:** 6tr, 12c, 28bl; **Courtesy of the National Security Agency:** 50bl; **Naval Historical Foundation, Washington, D.C.:** 11tr; **Nokia Corporation:** 27t/1, 27t/3, 27t/8; **Photolibrary:** Land of Lost Content 13tl, RubberBall 52r (Overlaid on to mobile phone), 53bl (inset); **Larry Press:** 44l/1, 44l/2, 44l/3, 44l/4; **Press Association Images:** Shizuo Kambayashi / AP 63br, Mark Lennihan 27t/6; **PunchStock:** 2cr, 54t; **Courtesy Rensselaer Polytechnic Institute Alumni:** 52tl; **Science Museum / Science & Society Picture Library:** 16cr, 46bl, 64-65c; **Science Photo Library:**

Massimo Brega, The Lighthouse 4bl, 59r, Andrew Brookes, National Physical Laboratory 51br, Michael Donne 19tr, Einstein@Home 46br, Equinox Graphics 59tr, European Space Agency / Aeos Medialab 57tl, Gustoimages 13br, James King-Holmes 50-51c, Hybrid Medical Animation 2-3t, 62-63c, Edward Kinsman 4br, 10-11, Hank Morgan 30-31, 31cr, Sam Ogden 61b, David Parker 29tl, Phillipe Plailly 31br, Victor de Schwanberg 34bc, Volker Steger 63tr, Sheila Terry 4tr, 14br, Catherine Ursillo 16bl; Evrim Sen: 2cla, 48cr; **U.S. Department of Energy, Oak Ridge National Laboratory:** 30-31b; **US Department of Defense:** 49br; **Ed Uthman:** 28c; **Voltage PR:** 40-41b; **Vincenzo Cosenza, www.vincos.it:** 66-67

Jacket: *Front:* **Alamy Images:** Nigel James tr; **Dorling Kindersley:** Sarah Ashun ca; **Getty Images:** ballyscanlon b, Gregor Schuster cla, SSPL ftl; **Samsung:** cra; *Back:* **Alamy Images:** Ian Patrick tr, sciencephotos ca; **Getty Images:** Thomas Northcut bc; **Science Photo Library:** Massimo Brega, The Lighthouse bl, Hank Morgan cra, br

Wallchart: Corbis: Ed Kashi ftr, Patrick van Katwijk clb; **Dorling Kindersley: The Science Museum** fcla; **Getty Images:** Glowimages cl; **Honda (UK):** bl; **Museum of Natural Sciences, Brussels:** tl; **Science Photo Library:** Massimo Brega, The Lighthouse cb, James King-Holmes fcra, Edward Kinsman cla, Sam Ogden br, Sheila Terry fcl; **US Department of Defense:** cra; **Voltage PR:** cr

All other images © Dorling Kindersley
For further information see: www.dkimages.com